NEW REVISED EDITION

THE COMPLETE ENERGY-SAVING HOME IMPROVEMENT GUIDE

SAVE UP TO 50% OF YOUR HOME FUEL COST

Edited by James W. Morrison

Arco Publishing, Inc.
New York

ACKNOWLEDGEMENTS

The facts and material in this book are based on the findings and methods published in these Federal Government reports: *Retrofitting Existing Housing for Energy Conservation: An Economic Analysis* and *Making the Most of Your Energy Dollars* by the Commerce Department's National Bureau of Standards, the Federal Energy Administration's "Project Retrotech," the Department of Housing and Urban Development's *In the Bank . . . Or Up the Chimney?*, the Office of Economic Opportunity's *Save Energy: Save Money, Home Winterization: A Technical Report,* by the Office of State Planning and Energy, Department of Administration, State of Wisconsin, *Passive Design Ideas for the Energy Conscious Consumer* by the National Solar Heating and Cooling Information Center (U.S. Department of Housing and Urban Development in cooperation with U.S. Department of Energy), "Heating with Wood" from the Northeast Regional Agricultural Engineering Services of the Northeast Land Grant Universities and the U.S. Department of Agriculture, and "The Creosote Problem" from the Energy Saving Series (#3) of the New Hampshire Extension Service.

LEGAL NOTICE

Reference to trade names or specific commercial products, commodities, or services in this manual does not represent or constitute an endorsement, recommendation, or favoring by ARCO of the specific commercial product, commodity, or service. ARCO and the editor are not responsible and disclaim liability for any results or lack of results that may or may not accrue from the adoption or failure to adopt any of the suggestions set forth in this manual. ARCO and the editor do not warrant the achievement of any cost savings and disclaim liability for the failure to achieve any cost savings as a result of the following of any suggestions set forth herein.

All items mentioned in this manual will contribute to efficient energy use. There is no way to guarantee a specific dollar saving on fuel bills. Since fuel costs will continue to rise and lifestyles and conditions of existing houses differ widely, only average estimated percentages of savings can be indicated for all items mentioned. However, a properly retrofitted house will require a smaller energy input than the same house before it was retrofitted.

DEDICATION
For Ed Turner, who always worked for Arco and always dedicated himself to the good of mankind.

Third Edition, First Printing, 1979

Published by Arco Publishing Inc.
219 Park Avenue South, New York, N.Y. 10003

Copyright © 1979 by Arco Publishing Inc.

Portions of this book were published in government pamphlets entitled *In the Bank . . . Or Up the Chimney?*, *Solar Hot Water and Your Home*, *Project Retrotech*, *Home Heating in an Emergency*, *Home Winterization: A Technical Report*, and *Passive Design Ideas for the Energy Conscious Consumer*.

All rights reserved.

Library of Congress Cataloging in Publication Data

Arco Publishing , New York.
    The complete energy-saving home improvement guide.

    1. Dwellings — Energy conservation. I. Title.

TJ163.5.D86A73   1979   697   79-64055
ISBN 0-668-04808-5 (Paper Edition)

Printed in the United States of America

Preface

To American Homeowners:

Undoubtedly, you no longer need to be told that the cost of heating and cooling your home is taking a much bigger bite out of your budget than ever before. Where can you, the homeowner, turn for reliable, understandable information to help you put dollars in the bank instead of up the chimney?

Energy-saving techniques applicable to those types were gathered and compared as to cost and potential fuel savings. The comparison was designed to emphasize safe and cost-saving energy conservation techniques that would return the greatest practical net savings to the homeowner over the life of the investment. This book will help you to grasp quickly the essential energy-saving techniques that your home may require and to choose wisely between do-it-yourself projects and contractor services.

Step-by-step installation instructions for each energy-saving method described are combined with illustrations that can take the mystery out of seemingly complex tasks. Detailed but easy forms enable you to compute the cost-savings of each method to help you save dollars and cents in home energy expenditures. When that happens, you will benefit—and our country will reduce its consumption of precious fuels.

You know that energy prices are still on the rise. That's why *now* is the time to invest in energy conserving measures that will help lower your costs in home heating and cooling operations. After all, saving energy means saving money.

Household energy costs can be reduced with relatively simple home improvements. Installing or adding insulation, storm windows, and doors and applying weather stripping and caulking are important. But how much insulation is enough? When are storm windows and storm doors good investments?

This book is designed to take the confusion and guesswork out of home energy conservation practices. Using the worksheets in the Job Book you can determine the best combination of improvements for *your* house, climate, and fuel costs—improvements that will provide the largest long run savings in your home heating and cooling expenses.

If you are a homeowner who wants to save energy and money without sacrificing comfort, this book is for you. It is a "how-to" and a "how much" guide to energy conservation investments. Making the most of your energy dollars is the only way a money conscious homeowner can evaluate the costs and investments in order to offset rising energy prices. If you follow this guide you will be saving money and at the same time doing your part to help conserve our nation's precious energy supplies.

J.W.M.

TAXPAYER'S NOTE

Under the National Energy Act of 1978, taxpayers receive tax credits for installing energy-saving materials in their homes amounting to 15 percent of the first $2,000 spent on qualifying equipment, up to a maximum of $300. The credit can be subtracted from taxes due.

The credit could be applied to any equipment installed after April 20, 1977, the day President Carter announced his energy plan. The credit would be for existing dwellings only (in existence as of the effective date of the act). The credit would be effective through Dec. 31, 1985. The installation must be made in the taxpayer's principal residence. Eligible for the credit are owners, renters, and owners of cooperatives or condominiums.

A taxpayer who qualified for a tax credit in excess of the tax he owes could carry the credit forward on future tax returns through the taxable years ending Jan 1, 1988. However, for expenditures made in 1977, a credit could only be claimed on the taxpayer's 1978 tax return. Be sure to check with the local office of the Internal Revenue Service before applying for a tax credit for energy saving improvements. For further information on the recommended criteria for retrofit materials and products eligible for tax credit write to: U.S. Department of Energy, Federal Building, 400 First Street, N.W., Washington, D.C. 20545. Request publication NBSIR 75-795 or the latest copy of the recommended criteria for retrofitting one- and two-family residences.

Contents

PART 1: PASSIVE ENERGY DESIGN FOR THE ENERGY CONSCIOUS CONSUMER

■ Introduction

AN ENERGY CONSCIOUS HOME is one which goes beyond conventional energy conserving features such as insulation in the right places, double glazing and weatherstripping at all openings. It incorporates passive design ideas and/or solar energy systems in its planning, design, construction and use.

This booklet introduces you to some of these ideas and approaches—approaches which not only produce additional energy savings, but which also make use of solar energy in a passive way. Whether you presently own a home, or whether you plan to build one, you will find many of the ideas presented here of value.

What Do We Mean By "Passive Design Ideas"?

Passive design ideas or approaches,
■ use solar energy naturally,
■ contain little mechanical hardware,
■ require little or no energy themselves, and
■ tend to be low in cost.

Sometimes it's easiest to understand passive ideas by contrasting them with "active" design examples. Furnaces, boilers, electric water heaters and air conditioners all fall into the active area: they require complex, expensive and energy-consuming equipment. An active approach to solar heating and cooling uses a carefully-designed, complex and sophisticated solar collector, with fans, pumps, storage or heat exchange units and sophisticated controls. In contrast, one passive approach to solar heating or cooling is a regular window, of the right size, with the right orientation to the sun, designed to capture natural breezes, with insulated window shutter and sufficient heat storage mass.

What Is An Energy Conscious Home?

An energy conscious home approaches the conservation of energy through passive design ideas, and through the use of solar energy, in its planning, design, construction and use. Location, configuration, orientation to the sun and breezes, layout, method of construction, and particular design details are all carefully considered.

Like the better energy conserving homes now being constructed and renovated around the country, the energy conscious home is well insulated, and incorporates double glazing and weatherstripping where they are needed—but it goes well beyond that. And its energy savings go well beyond those found in conventional homes, too.

Using Part I

This part sketches a number of passive design approaches and ideas. For each approach, it shows one or two ways of incorporating it into homes (there are many more approaches which can be taken), and in most cases it indicates a possible ENERGY SAVINGS (expressed as a percentage reduction).

The energy savings figure is an important one. It is derived by comparing the heating energy used in the design shown with a more conventional design of a 1,600 square foot "standard practice home" located in a region with a fairly cold climate, such as that found in upstate New York. The standard practice home already incorporates good current practice (insulation, weatherstripping, double glazing, 65° winter thermostat settings).

Making The Decision

The passive design ideas in this are a diverse group, and many may not apply to your situation:
■ Some make more sense in cold climates, and others in warmer climates.
■ Some can be incorporated into existing homes—these are clearly marked with an asterisk—and others are applicable only in new construction.
■ Some may appeal to you, and others may not.

It is up to you to select those passive design ideas which you may wish to consider in your home. Hopefully, this raises your own energy consciousness and stimulates you to consider some of the ideas shown. The booklet, though, provides only quick sketches; you may want to consult with architects, builders or developers who have the technical resources to do a more complete job of determining the full impact of these ideas in YOUR situation.

Some of the passive design ideas presented here have a significant impact on the design of the house. The examples presented here are only illustrative. If you are intrigued with the idea,

please don't consider the design solution shown here the "only way to go".

We suggest that, once you have pinpointed those approaches which are of interest to you, you consult a number of architects or builders. They are in a position to discuss the specific implications of these ideas for you and your situation—including specific energy savings and impacts on building cost.

■ It Begins With the Site

Energy conscious design begins with choosing a site which offers opportunities to conserve energy as well as to capture energy from the sun and cooling breezes for heating and cooling your home. Here are some suggestions:

South-Facing Glass Facade

To capture solar energy, face your main living areas to the south and provide sufficient glass area to allow the solar radiation to enter.

Once the solar radiation enters it has to be stored, retained or prevented from being lost through the walls. There are numerous ways of storing and retaining this solar energy. The building's walls, floors, and ceilings can act as storage devices, as can furniture and special heat storage components.

Orientation for Natural Ventilation

You can use prevailing summer breezes to cool your home. The ideal orientation of the side of the house through which the breezes should enter is an oblique angle of 20° to 70° between the wall and wind direction. This will maximize the natural ventilation in the interior. Call your local weather bureau to obtain the prevailing wind direction in your area.

However, locating the house is always a compromise between south facing windows for heating in the winter, and capturing the breezes for cooling in the summer. To protect your facades from winter winds, locate evergreens, fences, and earth berms on the north and west side of your home.

If you are located on a hill and/or near a lake, the following additional rules are relevant:

■ Near a body of water, breezes move from the water to the land during the day, and flow in reverse at night.

■ On a south-facing hill, breezes tend to move up the hill during the day, and downhill at night.

No matter how your home is sited, you can increase natural ventilation and cooling by using casement-type windows, or partially-opened shutters, on the windward side of the building. These projections create mini-pressure zones in front of the window openings, and increase the velocity of the breeze passing into the openings.

General Rules

When designing with these concepts in mind, there are some general guidelines that you may use in making appropriate decisions. How you use the site relates to several other factors.

- SOUTH-FACING GLASS. To capture the necessary solar radiation, it is necessary to provide a minimum amount of south-facing glass. The minima: 1/4 to 1/5 of the floor area (in temperate climates); 1/3 to 1/4 of the floor area (in colder climates). Combined with proper heat storage mass and insulating shutters, these glass areas can provide 50% or more of the building's space heating needs in warmer climates.

- HEAT STORAGE. Heat may be stored in containers filled with water, masonry walls and floors, flower boxes, rock or sand beds, and even furniture. The storage capacity required depends on the amount of radiation captured and the building's use characteristics. In temperate climates, for example, it is necessary to provide 30 pounds of water or 150 pounds of rock storage for each square foot of south-facing glass. If the storage medium cannot be directly exposed to the sun, this number will have to be increased by as much as four times. The ratios of floor area and heat storage surface area should be a minimum of 1:1 to gain the maximum benefit of passive solar heating.

- SHADING. To prevent excess heat gain in the summer, provide window shading. These devices (overhangs, grilles, awnings, etc.) should shade the total glass area at noon during the hottest months. Careful attention to orientation and the sun's path through the sky will be required during design. For additional shading, use deciduous trees on the south side of the house: they block the summer sun while allowing the winter sun to penetrate.

- SHUTTERS. To prevent heat loss at night, insulated shutters should be closed over the glass areas. During the summer the process can be reversed to gain some cooling: close the shutters during the day, open them at night, exposing the glass areas to the cool night.

■ What Type Of House Saves Energy?

People have different tastes in housing: some of us like split ranch, some the two-story colonial, while others prefer more contemporary design. Irrespective of style, however, the shape and overall volume of your house can contribute to savings—or excesses—when it comes to energy consumption. Shape and volume can also maximize the use of solar energy through passive means.

To provide some basis for comparison, let's use a basic STANDARD PRACTICE HOUSE which is not unlike many single-family homes being built and occupied around the country today.

Standard Practice House

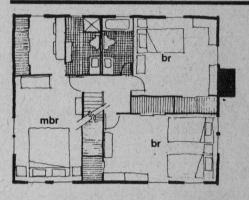

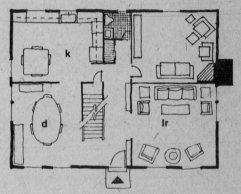

The Standard Practice House has 1,600 square feet of living space on two floors, as well as a full basement. It already includes conventional energy-conserving features such as full insulation, storm windows and weatherstripping.

To illustrate the energy savings possible for each passive design idea, we first modify the Standard Practice House to incorporate it—WITHOUT changing its floor area or complement of rooms. Then we calculate the amount of heating—and sometimes cooling—energy required. Comparing the energy required in the modified Standard Practice House to that required before the modification was introduced gives us a percentage energy saving, and this figure is included with each passive design idea. All calculations are based on the assumption that the house is located in a cold region such as upstate New York.

One Story
Rectangular House   4%†

A large amount of the total heat loss in a home during the winter occurs through exterior walls—and particularly through and around windows and doors in those walls. Reconfiguring the Standard Practice House into a one-story rectangle does several things:

- The total exterior wall area is reduced.
- The interior rooms have less exposure to the outside, and window area is also reduced somewhat.
- Roof area is increased. In conventional construction it is possible to include more insulation in the roof than in the walls, thus further reducing heat loss. This is not to suggest that all one-story homes are more energy conscious than two-story homes. Trading wall area for roof area, however, can save heating energy.

---

†The percentage figure indicates the reduction in energy consumption compared to the STANDARD PRACTICE HOUSE.

If reducing wall area can save energy, then it follows that it makes sense to minimize the PERIMETER of the house. Consider the next two approaches.

Circular
Floor Plan   9%

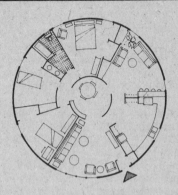

The smallest perimeter for a given area is a circle; this in turn gives us the minimum exterior surface area and the savings indicated.

Some, however, do not like round houses or find it awkward to accommodate their life styles in them. The next best alternative is the square floor plan; it saves energy, but not as much as the round plan.

One Story
Square Floor Plan   5%

Windows can contribute between 15% to 35% of the total heating energy lost in a house; so placing them strategically can make a significant difference in both reducing heat-loss and maximizing solar gain. To illustrate this point, let's stay with our square configuration floor plan and see what happens if we take the windows and face them into an atrium which is covered with a skylight.

Square Plan With Atrium   21%

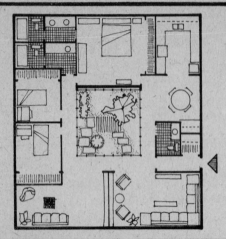

This plan includes the same floor and window area as the original Standard Practice House, but the windows are exposed to the inner atrium instead of to the exterior. The atrium is unheated, but because of the skylight, its winter temperature is not as low as that outside.

The energy savings shown results only from the reduction in heat loss through the windows and walls. The savings can be doubled or tripled if the atrium is also used (with insulated shutters) as a passive solar collector. The atrium design shown can also be used to reduce heat gain in warm weather if proper sun control and shading devices are used.

The important lesson from these examples is that minimum surface and window areas can save large amounts of energy. Further, locating windows for passive solar collection can significantly increase those savings.

■ Using Earth To Save Energy

Earth, like most other materials, does provide some thermal resistance, but in principle earth is not a good insulator. The benefit of earth is derived from its capacity to moderate temperature change. Earth slows down the temperature variations between interior and exterior, and it provides protection from cold winter winds. Thus it can contribute a great deal to reducing a building's heat loss.

One important thing to keep in mind is that with earth you must use insulation—in this case placed between the earth cover and the exterior of the structure. This arrangement gives the walls, roofs and ceilings the heat-storage capacity previously described.

To illustrate the impact of working with earth, let

us go back to our Standard Practice House. There, all the bedrooms were on the second floor; in the illustration below, they have been relocated below the first floor in what used to be the basement.

Bedrooms Below Finished Grade   23%

In doing this, the amount of excavation is not increased, but the first floor is raised slightly to maintain a 7'-6" ceiling height and to accommodate 2' high clerestory windows in the "under-the-ground" floor level. This makes the space much more liveable and saves considerable energy since much of the exterior wall is exposed to earth rather than to the outside. In the summertime, or in warm climates, this approach also reduces heat gain, requiring less cooling energy.

Another approach to using earth is to berm it up against the walls of the house. When conventional windows, say with 3' high sills, are used, earth can be bermed to the first-floor sills as shown for both the Standard Practice House and the Square Plan House.

Earth Berming to Window-Sill in Standard Practice House   7%

Earth Berming to Window-Sill, Square Plan   13%

Earth Berming to Roof Eave   32%

If clerestory windows can be used, and earth bermed to their sills, additional savings are possible. The temperature 4' to 5' below grade is relatively constant at around 55°F, and a duct located in the berm, with a small fan, provides a simple passive cooling system!

It should be noted that earth-berming and the introduction of below-grade spaces in houses requires careful attention to waterproofing, foundation drainage, means of egress and humidity control. Further, earth berming existing buildings requires special design and technical expertise: treatment of existing surfaces for protection from moisture, rodents, insects and even tree roots is required. Consult an expert for these applications.

The prospect of energy savings in underground houses is now becoming well known. This

approach not only saves heating energy but also offers an excellent way to keep cool without an air conditioning system in warmer climates.

■ Some Other Exterior Features

Having illustrated how plan, configuration, window placement and earth can contribute to energy savings through passive design, let's move on to some other exterior features which can produce energy savings.

Entry Lock Within Standard Practice House   7%

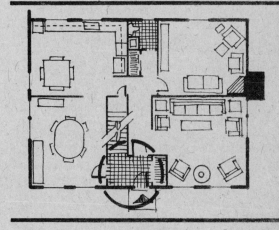

Entry Lock Added to Standard Practice House   5%

Doors are important penetrations in exterior walls, and where they open directly into the interior of the house, large amounts of heated or cooled air may escape each time they are opened. An entry lock, either designed into the interior of the house or added to the exterior, reduces energy loss by providing two doors (only one of which is normally open at any moment) separated by a small unheated or uncooled air space.

The Bead-Window   34%

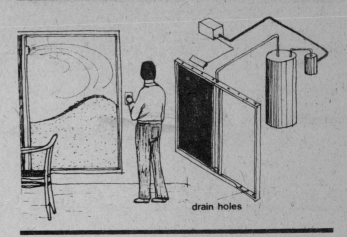

drain holes

The Greenhouse
heat-loss 8%
heat-gain 7%

One of the advantages of a greenhouse is that it allows the seasonal use of plants and shades to control heat transfer. A more sophisticated approach, based on the patented "bead wall" concept looks at the window as a device with varying thermal resistance—depending on the need. The bead-window consists of two glass or plastic sheets separated by a 3" air space which can be filled with high thermal resistance styrofoam beads using a pump and blower system; then emptied of the beads using a vacuum system. The calculation assumes that the north windows of the Standard Practice House are eliminated and that bead windows are placed on the remaining three walls of the Standard Practice House. The windows are assumed to be "transparent" to heat gain during these hours:

■ East windows, transparent from 8 am to 11 am
■ South windows, transparent from 8 am to 4 pm
■ West windows, transparent from 1 pm to 4 pm.

Additional savings can be obtained by turning an entry lock into a greenhouse. The "greenhouse effect" is well known: solar radiation through large glass areas will keep temperatures at reasonable levels (even without supplementary heating) in the wintertime; by adding plants and other insulating/shading devices, the effects of high heat gain in warmer weather can be mitigated.

Adding a greenhouse to a home increases the thermal resistance of the outside envelope in two ways:

■ the 'outside' temperature of the main exterior wall is increased in cold weather and decreased in warm weather, and,
■ infiltration losses around doors and windows are reduced because the main wall no longer is directly exposed to the elements.

The energy savings shown result only from the increased thermal resistance of the envelope; using a greenhouse as a passive solar collector provides additional savings if it is oriented properly and if heat storage capability is included in its design.

Window Shutters
heat-loss 28%
heat-gain 34%

A more conventional approach to "adjusting" the thermal resistance of windows is to use shutters —IF they have genuine insulating value. The shutters shown have a wood face and an insulating core; once applied to the windows of the Standard Practice House, the savings shown result if they are opened on the following schedule:

- East wall, opened from 8 am-11 am (winter)
  1 pm-4 pm (summer)
- South wall, opened from 8 am-4 pm (winter)
  7-9 am; 3-5 pm (summer)
- West wall, opened from 1 pm-4 pm (winter)
  8 am-11 am (summer)
- North wall, opened from any three hours (winter)
  8 am-7 pm (summer)

Speaking of window shutters, it is possible to conceive of a window shutter which, in its open position, functions as a solar collector with a self-contained storage unit. When closed, the shutter/collector vents the stored heat directly into the room.

Solar Window Shutter

room savings . . . **54%**
house savings . . **6%**

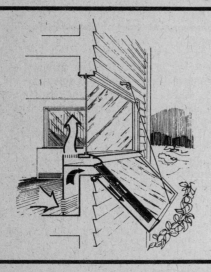

The hinged solar window shutter can be inclined to respond to the appropriate radiation angle and it can be closed against the window frame. The shutter retains the heat generated by solar radiation, and when closed, operable vents facilitate heat transfer into the room.

The calculation assumes the use of such shutters in one of the bedrooms of the Standard Practice House where one window faces east and another faces south. The second figure given indicates the impact of our example on the total energy consumption of the house.

Another approach to passive solar systems is to integrate a solar collector with the window assembly as shown. The collector incorporates collection, storage and direct venting into the interior room. To produce the savings indicated, the collector-windows are used in the southeast bedroom of the Standard Practice House.

Solar Window Unit 62%

Looking at solar collectors, it's possible to take passive design approaches to incorporating them into the home.

One approach is to integrate collectors into earth berming as shown. The berm angle should be the same as the average solar radiation angle for the locale. The collector unit is self-contained, and heat is transferred into the building by convection and by control of manually-operated vents.

Solar Collectors On Earth Berms

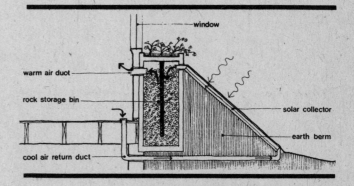

Earlier the importance of south-facing glass in capturing solar radiation was noted. In the illustrations shown here, the entire south-facing facade is treated as a "solar collector wall".
The first drawing depicts the principles behind the solar collector wall. Sun penetrating through the glass strikes the blackened surface of the masonry or concrete wall—simultaneously heat-

ing both the wall and the air space between the glass and the wall. The heated air in the space rises and enters the room at the top. Cool air enters at the bottom of the wall, to be heated in a continuous cycle (the principle is called "thermosyphoning"). In addition, the heat in the masonry wall migrates to the inside and, when the sun disappears, the wall acts as a radiator. Careful use of insulation allows use of the wall for cooling at night in the summer, too.

Vertical Solar Collector and Heat Storage Wall

The second drawing illustrates the conversion of the south facade of the Standard Practice Home to a solar collector wall. All of the doors and operable windows have been retained, however.

Solar
Collector Wall   27%

The Drum Wall

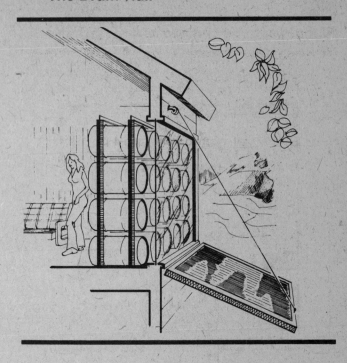

In a variation of the solar collector wall, the "drum wall" includes large drums of water placed in racks behind the window glass area. The exterior of the drum is painted black and the solar energy coming through the window is collected in the drums which, in turn, act as radiators to heat the room. At night large window shutters are closed over the outside of the glass area to prevent heat loss.

■ What Happens When You Put Some Of These Ideas Together?

So far we have dealt with a number of individual ideas—planning and design features which can reduce the amount of energy consumed in the home. What happens if you incorporate several of these features in your home?

As was pointed out earlier, energy savings from the passive design ideas shown are not necessarily additive. Each house presents its own situation—and requires its own energy consumption calculations.

To provide an illustration, let's take a number of the passive energy saving ideas and incorporate them into an ENERGY CONSCIOUS HOUSE.

Energy Conscious House Floor Plan	heat loss **32%**
	heat-gain . . . **23%**
	hot water . . . **36%**

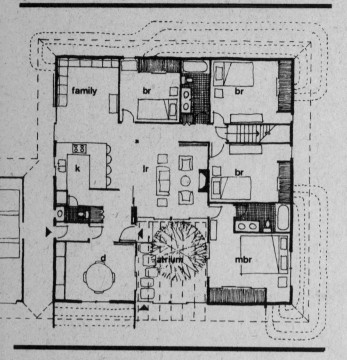

Energy Conscious House Perspective

The Energy Conscious House contains 1,600 square feet (excluding the atrium) and is analyzed under the same conditions as the earlier Standard Practice House. From the illustrations, you can see that the following features have been used:

- One-story Configuration
- Minimum Perimeter Distance
- Window Shutters
- Atrium and Entry Locks
- Earth Berming
- Maximum Insulation in Roof and Walls
- Weatherstripping and Storm Windows

Energy Conscious House Section

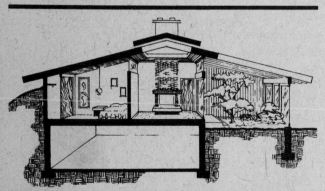

■ Summing Up

Energy conscious design can provide significant energy savings in homes. It begins with choosing the right site and properly locating the house to take advantage of the sun and wind as well as other natural forces. The house's configuration plan, exterior features and interior characteristics all contribute.

Most of the passive design ideas presented here are ready-to-implement; a few now exist only as concepts or prototypes. All can be considered in looking at new construction; many can also be incorporated into existing homes. Some, but not all, require special professional or technical expertise.

Which passive design approaches to consider? How much energy can you save? What will it cost?

There are no simple answers to these questions. Each home is unique. Your own needs, desires and priorities are critical factors in looking at your housing. Further, climatic conditions and construction approaches vary from place to place.

To optimize YOUR situation, it is suggested that you seek the assistance of an energy-conscious architect and/or builder early in the game. You can discuss your needs, your likes and dislikes, and your available resources. In return, you can gain information on expected costs and savings.

Energy consciousness now may reap significant —and continuing—dividends as you occupy your home year after year.

PART 2: HEAT LOSS CALCULATION

A Quick Quiz

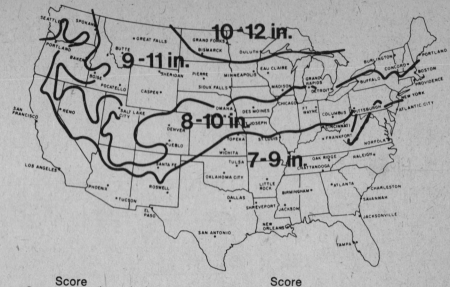

10-12 in.		
9-11 in.		
8-10 in.		
7-9 in.		

1. **What is Your Thermostat Setting?**
Score

If your thermostat is set at 68°F. or less during daytime in winter, score 6 points; 5 points for 69°; 4 points for 70°. If your thermostat is set above 70°, score 0. ___

If you have whole-house air conditioning and you keep your temperature at 78°F. in the summer, score 5 points; 4 points for 77°; 3 points for 76°. If you have no air conditioning, score 7 points. If your thermostat is set below 76°, score 0. ___

In winter, if you set your thermostat back to 60°F. or less at night, score 10 points; 9 points for 61°; 8 points for 62°; 7 points for 63°; 6 points for 64°; 5 points for 65°. If your thermostat is set above 65° at night, score 0. ___

2. **Is Your House Drafty?**
To check for drafts, hold a flame (candle or match) about 1 inch from where windows and doors meet their frames.
If the flame doesn't move, there is no draft around your windows, and you score 10 points. If the flame moves, score 0. ___

If there is no draft around your doors, add 5 points. If there is a draft, score 0. ___

If you have a fireplace and keep the damper closed or block the air flow when it is not in use, add 4 points. ___

If you do not have a fireplace, add 4 points. ___

If you leave the damper open when the fireplace is not being used, score 0. ___

3. **How Well is Your Attic Insulated?**
Check the map to determine the inches of ceiling insulation recommended for your zone.
If you already have the recommended thickness of insulation, score 30 points. ___

If you have 2 inches less insulation than you should, score 25 points. ___

If you have 4 inches less insulation than you should, score 15 points. ___
Score

If you have 6 inches less than you should, score 5 points. ___

If you have less than 2 inches of insulation in your attic, score 0. ___

4. **Is Your Floor Insulated?**
If you have unheated space under your house and there is insulation under your floor, add 10 points; if there is no insulation, score 0. ___

If you have a heated or air conditioned basement or if there is no space under your house, score 10. ___

5. **Do You Have Storm Windows?**
If you live in an area where the temperature frequently falls below 30°F. in winter and you use storm windows, score 20 points. If you do not have storm windows, score 0. ___

Your Energy Quotient: Total ___
How Well Did You Do?

How Well Did You Do?

90 or above: Congratulations! You are already an energy saver. By keeping your home well-insulated and draft-free, you are using energy more efficiently than 80 percent of your neighbors, based on the national average.

Under 90: You're spending more money than you need to in order to keep your home comfortable. Check the quiz again to see where you lost the most points. That's where you can make the greatest savings in your annual fuel bill, while improving the comfort, appearance, and resale value of your home as well.

Introduction to Heat Loss

Being comfortable in winter means keeping warm. This requires heat, which comes from increasingly expensive fuel. Most homes can use much less fuel without sacrificing comfort.

This manual explains the facts about winter comfort heating. It provides an easy method of approximating how much heat will be needed to keep any particular building warm and explains how to assess the benefits of improvements made to the building, such as adding storm windows, insulating exposed areas, excluding drafts.

Most such improvements cost money. Usually they save more than they cost. In the next few pages we shall see how to make heating improvements and how to figure the heat saved.

Most homes can use much less fuel without sacrificing comfort.

One important fact is that heat always tends to flow from a high-temperature area to a low-temperature area. For example, if you put a pan of cold water on a hot stove, the flow of heat from the stove through the bottom of the pan heats the water up to a higher temperature. Pan bottoms are, therefore, made of materials which conduct heat easily. To keep the pan from losing heat after it comes off the stove, you can stand it on an asbestos pad, a material that resists passage of heat or, in other words, provides insulation.

We put heat in a house to keep comfortable (and healthy) but the heat passes out of a house to the cold outside surroundings. If we want to keep the building at a comfortable temperature, we must control the actual heat-loss. Remember that the flow of air is always from hot to cold, and cold is really the absence of heat.

Begin your heat loss calculations with your ENERGY CONSUMPTION RECORD.

ENERGY CONSUMPTION RECORD

YEAR: _____

USING THIS FORM PROVIDES THE NECESSARY INFORMATION FOR "YOUR HOME WEATHERIZATION," PAGE 42, AND AS A BASIS FOR DEVELOPING CONTINUOUS RECORDS OF YOUR ENERGY USAGE.

MONTH	ELECTRICITY		FUEL CHECK: GAS OIL COAL	
	KWH	COST	QUANTITY	COST
JANUARY				
FEBRUARY				
MARCH				
APRIL				
MAY				
JUNE				
JULY				
AUGUST				
SEPTEMBER				
OCTOBER				
NOVEMBER				
DECEMBER				
TOTAL PER YEAR				

ANNUAL ENERGY CONSUMPTION IN HEATING UNITS

QUANTITY   HEATING UNITS

1. _____ KWH ÷ 30 = _____
   ELECTRICITY

2. _____ MCF* ÷ .12 = _____
   NATURAL GAS

3. _____ GAL ÷ 1.3 = _____
   OTHER GAS**

4. _____ GAL ÷ 1 = _____
   OIL

5. _____ LBS ÷ 15 = _____
   COAL

6. TOTAL HEATING UNITS................._____

*THOUSAND CUBIC FEET   **PROPANE, LPG OR BOTTLED GAS

Take the building below —

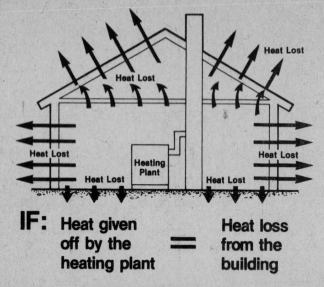

IF: Heat given
off by the   =   Heat loss
heating plant   from the
                     building

THEN: TEMPERATURE INSIDE
REMAINS CONSTANT

If a building has insulated walls, floors, and ceilings, double-glazed windows, and sealed cracks, then less heat will be needed to maintain comfortable temperatures inside the building. Less heat required means less fuel used, which means money saved.

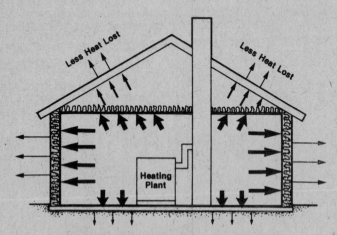

Less heat escaping means less heat and less fuel needed to stay comfortable inside

Heat escapes from a building in two ways: by conduction and by infiltration. In the next few pages, these processes will be explained — but first some definitions to make everything clear.

Introduction to Heat Loss

We must have a unit to measure heat losses. Normally we use the British Thermal Unit — Btu. This is the amount of heat it takes to raise the temperature of 1 pound of water by 1° Fahrenheit. Another way of "sizing" a Btu is to say it is about the amount of heat given off when a wooden match is burned completely. All fuel values or heat requirements can be expressed in Btu's: for example, using 1 kilowatt-hour of electricity releases 3,412 Btu; 1 pound of wood burned completely will give off about 8,000 Btu.

Working with Btu's means doing calculations with large numbers in which it is easy to make errors. This manual uses the concept of *Heating Units* to simplify the figuring —

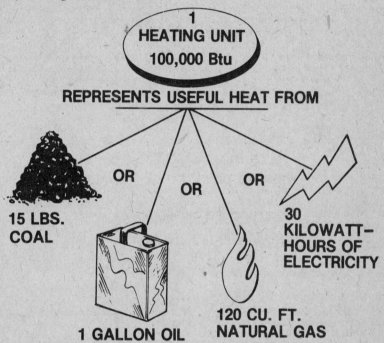

1 HEATING UNIT 100,000 Btu

REPRESENTS USEFUL HEAT FROM

15 LBS. COAL OR **1 GALLON OIL** OR **120 CU. FT. NATURAL GAS** OR **30 KILOWATT-HOURS OF ELECTRICITY**

Obviously, the *heating unit* is an approximation because not all oil or gas heating plants operate at the same efficiency. However, the *heating unit* is a fairly accurate estimate of what a normal oil or gas furnace should get out of the quantities of those fuels illustrated above. The heating unit does, in fact, represent about 100,000 Btu.

In this manual, we calculate heating requirements on a seasonal basis. Therefore, if a building is calculated to require 1,200 *heating units*, that figure represents the approximate number of gallons of oil it should use per year, if it has an efficient furnace. If the actual fuel use is known and is very different from the calculated figure, a further check needs to be made to find the reason. It may be due to calculation errors, wrong measurements in the building, or a poorly functioning furnace. It may be that the building has only been partially heated previously, with much of the living space not used in the winter. Working with *heating units* in this way can enable us to spot errors or circumstances we might otherwise miss. Incidentally, if the furnace which provides heat for the building also provides domestic hot water, this will increase the fuel use approximately 20 percent.
To allow for climatic differences between areas, heating engineers use degree-day figures: 1

degree-day represents a 24-hour period in which the average outside temperature is 1°F below a base temperature of 65°F. Many northern areas will have over 7,000 degree-days in a heating season. This manual uses the *district heating factor* which, for an area having 4,000 heating degree-days, will be 1, for 6,000 degree-days 1.5 and so on. The map on page 25 shows *district heating factors* for various areas. Simply look up the approximate factor for your area, and use it in figuring all heat losses for any house in your district.

Home weatherization requires four steps to determine what should be done, where, and how:

1. INSPECTION of the building to determine construction.
2. CALCULATION of heat losses from the building.
3. EVALUATION of the building and heat losses to determine what weatherization measures should be made.
4. INSTALLATION of the weatherization materials.

A job book is used for recording the information on each building. It also shows the procedure for calculating and summarizing heat loss and serves as an order form for listing and procuring materials.

Heat is lost from the home through the exterior surface of the building as heat flows by conduction through the building materials. The rate of heat loss from the warm side to the cold side through the exterior surface depends on the size of the surface, the length of time the heat flow occurs, the temperature difference between the two sides of the exposed area, and the construction of the section (the type of material used in the construction). All materials used in building construction reduce the flow of heat. Some materials are much better than others at reducing heat flow. The more effective materials are used as insulation. A well-insulated building will also stay cooler in the summer.

TYPES OF INSULATION

Three general types in insulation materials are commonly used in building construction. They are loose fill, blanket or batt, and rigid insulation.

Loose fill include such types of insulation as glass, rockwool, cellulose fibers, and wood fibers. Fill type insulating materials are best utilized on horizontal surfaces, such as ceiling areas. This type of insulation used in vertical areas tends to settle, and unless provision is made to refill the space, cold spots can occur.

Blanket, or **batt insulation**, is commonly made of glass, rockwool, or wood fiber. They are usually enclosed in a paper envelope or fastened to a backing of kraft paper or aluminum foil. Some blanket types of insulation have no backing and are intended to be used when no vapor barrier is required. Blanket insulation comes in rolls of various lengths and thicknesses. Batt insulation is usually thicker and comes in shorter lengths. Both blanket and batt insulation are available for framing spacing of 16 and 24 inches. Other widths are available on special order.

Rigid insulation, in addition to providing insulating value, also provides structural strength. Rigid insulation is available in board form, such as various fiberboard materials and foamed plastics. Rigid insulation is used quite extensively by contractors and not individual homeowners. In some instances, this type insulation is less expensive.

Table 1 lists the insulating value of most of the common material found in house construction. The R value shown in the right-hand column indicates the effectiveness, or resistance value of the material. *The higher the resistance value, the better the insulating quality.* When building sections are made of several materials, the resistance value of each of the individual materials can be added together to obtain the overall total resistance value. Once you know the overall R value you can use it in the calculation outlined in the job book to determine heat loss. Thicknesses of 3½ inches (R-11) and 6 inches (R-19) are most common.

Vapor Barriers

In the winter, moisture moves from the inside of the home to the outside through the exterior surfaces. Vapor barriers are installed to reduce the flow of moisture through the insulation so that condensation will not occur. Blanket or batt insulation usually has vapor barriers attached. Polyethylene film (4 mils thick) can be used as a separate vapor barrier if needed. Vapor barriers should always be installed on the warm side (inside) to stop the moisture before it reaches the insulation. If possible, vent the cold side of the insulation to the outside to remove moisture which escapes through the insulation. When a blanket or batt insulation having an attached vapor barrier is used, kraft paper backing is usually cheaper than foil backing. If foil backing is used, a ¾" to 3" clearance is necessary in order to maintain effectiveness.

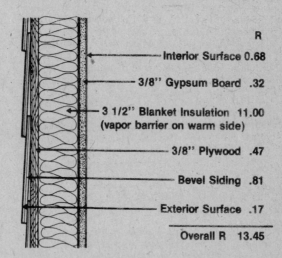

	R
Interior Surface	0.68
3/8" Gypsum Board	.32
3 1/2" Blanket Insulation (vapor barrier on warm side)	11.00
3/8" Plywood	.47
Bevel Siding	.81
Exterior Surface	.17
Overall R	**13.45**

Exterior Walls

To determine the insulating value of an exterior wall section, it is necessary to know the construction of the wall. Using Table 1, determine the R value for each material making up the wall. Add together these values to obtain the overall R value of the wall.

Building Heat Loss by Conduction

Ceilings and Roofs

The insulating value of roof and ceiling sections can be determined by adding the R value of each of the materials making up the section. It is necessary to know the construction of the ceiling or roof section. Add together the R values of the materials making up the section from the values given in Table 1 to obtain the overall R value of the section. For ceilings having attic space over the insulation, use an interior surface resistance for the surface next to the attic due to the fact that still air conditions exist on the outside of the insulation. The illustration shows the procedure for determining the overall resistance value for ceiling sections.

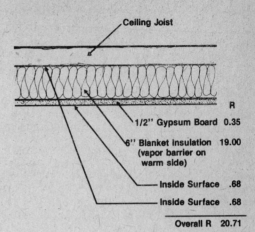

	R
1/2" Gypsum Board	0.35
6" Blanket insulation (vapor barrier on warm side)	19.00
Inside Surface	.68
Inside Surface	.68
Overall R	20.71

For roof sections, the procedure to determine overall resistance value is similar to that for the wall section. First, determine the construction of the roof section, and then add the resistance of the individual materials making up the roof section to obtain the overall R value for the roof. The diagram at the right shows the procedure for determining the overall R value for roof areas.

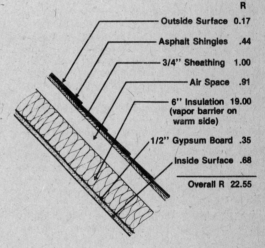

	R
Outside Surface	0.17
Asphalt Shingles	.44
3/4" Sheathing	1.00
Air Space	.91
6" Insulation (vapor barrier on warm side)	19.00
1/2" Gypsum Board	.35
Inside Surface	.68
Overall R	22.55

Floors

To determine the insulating value of floors, add the R value of the individual materials making up the floor section together to determine the overall R value. Use the interior surface resistance for the surface next to the basement or crawl space area. The heat loss from floors depends on the temperature below the floor. Basement and crawl space temperatures depend on the quality of construction. In calculating floor heat loss in this manual, a floor exposure factor is used to estimate changes in floor heat loss due to different types of foundation construction.

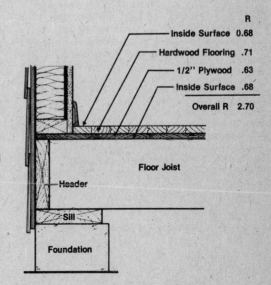

	R
Inside Surface	0.68
Hardwood Flooring	.71
1/2" Plywood	.63
Inside Surface	.68
Overall R	2.70

This list is not intended to include all types of building materials, but only materials commonly used in residences. If necessary, select the material most similar, and the resulting values will not substantially affect the calculation.

Table 1: Insulation Value of Common Materials

MATERIAL	THICKNESS (Inches)	R VALUE
Air Film and Spaces:		
Air space, bounded by ordinary materials	¾ or more	.91
Air space, bounded by aluminum foil	¾ or more	2.17
Exterior surface resistance	—	.17
Interior surface resistance	—	.68
Masonry:		
Sand and gravel concrete block	8	1.11
	12	1.28
Lightweight concrete block	8	2.00
	12	2.13
Face brick	4	.44
Concrete cast in place	8	.64
Building Materials — General:		
Wood sheathing or subfloor	3/4	1.00
Fiber board insulating sheathing	3/4	2.10
Plywood	5/8	.79
	1/2	.63
	3/8	.47
Bevel-lapped siding	1/2 x 8	.81
	3/4 x 10	1.05
Vertical tongue and groove board	3/4	1.00
Drop siding	3/4	.94
Asbestos board	1/4	.13
3/8" gypsum lath and 3/8" plaster	3/4	.42
Gypsum board (sheet rock)	3/8	.32
Interior plywood panel	1/4	.31
Building paper	—	.06
Vapor barrier	—	.00
Wood shingles	—	.87
Asphalt shingles	—	.44
Linoleum	—	.08
Carpet with fiber pad	—	2.08
Hardwood floor	—	.71
Insulation Materials (mineral wool, glass wool, wood wool):		
Blanket or batts	1	3.70
	3 1/2	11.00
	6	19.00
Loose fill	1	3.33
Rigid insulation board (sheathing)	3/4	2.10
Windows and Doors:		
Single window	—	approx. 1.00
Double window	—	approx. 2.00
Exterior door	—	approx. 2.00

Source: **ASHRAE** Guide and Data Book.

Building Heat Loss by Infiltration

Any building will constantly exchange air with its environment: outside air leaks in, inside air leaks out. A certain amount of this exchange (say, one complete air change per hour) is necessary for ventilation, but most buildings have much more than is needed. In winter, the air that leaks in is cold; the air that leaks out is warm; fuel is used to supply this temperature difference. Exfiltration (the flow of air is always from hot to cold) is the main reason for a cold house.

This leakage or infiltration is caused by wind, the building acting as a chimney, and the opening of outside doors.

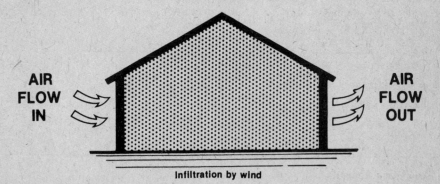

AIR FLOW IN

AIR FLOW OUT

Infiltration by wind

The effect of door openings and wind needs little explanation, but the chimney effect may not be obvious. When air in a building is warmer than the outside air, the entire building acts like a chimney — hot air tends to rise and leak out of cracks at the upper levels and sucks cold air in through cracks at the lower levels. Both the temperature difference and building height contribute to this effect. A two-story house having a 68°F inside temperature and a 30°F outside temperature will produce a "chimney" leakage equivalent to a 10 mile per hour wind blowing against the building.

EXFILTRATION

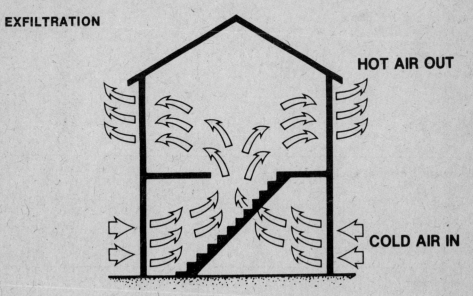

HOT AIR OUT

COLD AIR IN

"Chimney Effect"

Each cubic foot of air that enters the house requires approximately 0.02 Btu to raise the temperature 1°F. To determine the heat loss from infiltration, it is necessary to know the rate of air movement through the home. Most houses undergo from one to three air changes per hour, depending on construction. An infiltration checklist is provided to determine the approximate infiltration rate.

DISTRICT HEATING FACTOR FOR THE UNITED STATES

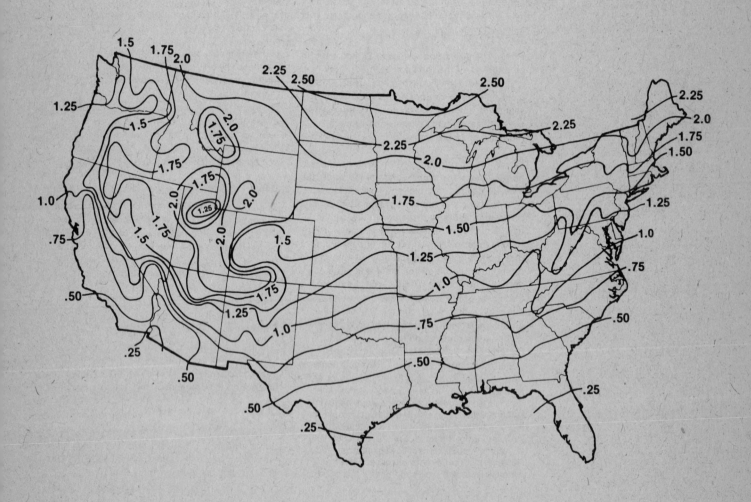

Home Weatherization in Four Steps

Step 1: Inspection of Building

When You Visit the House

A thorough inspection of the house is necessary in order to find out the information necessary for determining weatherization measures. Check the house as thoroughly as possible, and make sure that all the details described below are collected before you leave. If you find unusual building construction, location, arrangement, or other features that need to be taken into consideration, make notes on page 42 of the job book for future reference.

1. *Measure the outside of the house, the length, the width, the height of the sidewalls.* Draw a sketch of each side of the house and a floor plan on page 41 of the job book. Note the dimensions. It is not necessary that you measure the building to the last inch. If you find that you do not have access to some of the dimensions, estimate as closely as possible. You will find that it is accurate enough for your calculations.

2. *Check the doors and windows.* Sketch them in on page 41 of the job book in their proper location; note their construction, using an **S** for a single window or door and **D** for a double window or door. If you do not have access to a window, estimate its dimensions. Otherwise, measure and note the sizes in the job book.

3. *Check the construction of the exterior of the home.* Check the construction of the walls, the exterior ceiling, and roof and floor surfaces. It is necessary to know what kind of materials make up these areas in order to determine how well they are insulated. If you cannot readily determine this, ask the occupants. If they do not know, then you may be able to find out by taking off a switch plate or a plate over an outlet box on the exterior wall to examine the inside of the wall. However, if you have difficulty finding what is in the wall or ceiling, chances are that you cannot do anything about it. Once you have found the construction materials for the exterior surface, list the construction materials in the job book under "Walls, ceiling and roof, or floors" (pages 44, 45, and 48). Note the material and thickness of the material so that you can later determine its insulating value. Note also if you can get access to the area where the insulation will have to be installed. If, for instance, a wall is enclosed with sheathing material, it is difficult to add insulation. However, if you have an attic space over an accessible ceiling, you can insulate the ceiling.

4. *Check the building foundation to determine the floor exposure factor on page 31 of job book.* Put a checkmark in the box opposite the foundation description that best describes the actual building foundation.

5. *Check the condition of the home to determine the approximate infiltration rate.* Put a checkmark in the box under category 1, 2, or 3 that best describes the condition of each building component in the table on page 23 of the job book. In order to select the appropriate category, check for the following:

Building Foundation

To determine leakage around sills and cellar windows, examine the structure from the inside. Look for daylight between the sill and the foundation. Feel for drafts at cellar windows. Push on windows to see if they are loose or rattle. Check for missing putty on sash. This detailed analysis will help decide if the cellar is in category 1, 2, or 3.

If the building is on posts, infiltration must be evaluated by an examination of the floor. Open kitchen floor cabinets, and look at pipe holes for the sink drain. If these are tight, the building is category 1; if very open, category 3. Check the construction of the floor: if made of plywood or subfloor, paper, and finished floor, check category 1; if board floor having visible cracks and discernible drafts, check category 3.

Doors

Open the door quickly—a good fit will create a vacuum and resist the effort to open. A loose door will offer very little resistance. An on-hands-and-knees examination of the crack between the door and sill will also help. If a 25-cent piece can be pushed under the door, check category 2; if two 25-cent pieces can be used, check category 3.

Windows

The same evaluation can be used on windows (push hard on the window): if a 25-cent piece can be pushed between the window and the casing, check category 2; if two can be used, check category 3.

Walls

To determine infiltration through the walls, feel for drafts around outside wall electrical outlets. Check for caulking around doors and windows, condition of paint, and building paper.

The following are typical features of buildings having infiltration rates of approximately 1, 2, or 3 air changes per hour:

Building Component	One Air Change Per Hour	Two Air Changes Per Hour	Three Air Changes Per Hour
Building with cellar OR	Tight, no cracks, caulked sills, sealed cellar windows, no grade entrance leaks	Some foundation cracks, no weatherstripping on cellar windows, grade entrance not tight	Stone foundation, considerable leakage area, poor seal around grade entrance
Building with crawl space or on posts	Plywood floor, no trap door leaks, no leaks around water, sewer and electrical openings	Tongue and groove board floor, reasonable fit on trap doors, around pipes, etc.	Board floor, loose fit around pipes, etc.
Windows	Storm windows with good fit	No storm windows, good fit on regular windows	No storm windows, loose fit on regular windows
Doors	Good fit on storm doors	Loose storm doors, poor fit on inside door	No storm doors, loose fit on inside door
Walls	Caulked windows and doors, building paper used under siding	Caulking in poor repair	No indication of building paper, evident cracks around door and window frame

Usually building components are not all in the same infiltration category. You can estimate the approximate rate by considering how many of the components are in each category. For example, if two components are in the three air-change category and two are in the two air-change category, the overall infiltration would be 2½ air changes per hour.

6. Talk with the occupant of the house. Get his comments on the weatherization problems and what he thinks can be done about them. Note his comments on page 42 of the job

book. You may find more problems with the building by talking with the occupant than by looking at the house.

7. If you can, get answers to the questions on page 42 of the job book.

8. Before you leave, fill in the directions for locating the house, either by map or description of how to get there, on page 50 of the job book. This will help the person who is to do the work on the house.

The next step in the home weatherization procedure is to calculate the heat losses expected from the house. Only simple calculations are necessary, and you can do it away from the job site. By following the job book step by step, you can calculate the amount of heat lost in a given season from the building. To do this, you must determine the area of the exposed surface where the heat is lost; determine its insulation (R) value, select the district heating factor from the map on page 25 of the manual, determine the infiltration rate from the table on page 43 of the job book, and from these figures you are able to calculate the

heat loss from the building. On each of the pages of the job book, calculate the heat loss and the potential heat loss for infiltration losses, losses from windows and doors, floors, ceilings or roof, and walls, and summarize these heat losses on page 49 in the job book.

If you are unable to determine the construction of the exposed area and its heat loss, note that on the appropriate job sheet, and also note it in the summary sheet. You are now ready to determine what weatherization measures should be taken on the house.

Home Weatherization in Four Steps
Step 3: Evaluation of Data

Determining Weatherization Measures

In order to determine which weatherization measures should be undertaken on the home, we need to consider several factors. By following the step-by-step procedure listed below, you should be able to determine the logical areas where weatherization should be undertaken.

1. *Check the heat units* now required on the first column of the summary sheet, page 49 of the job book. Look for areas that have the highest heat requirement as logical areas for weatherization.

2. *Check the owner's comments* on the bottom of page 42 of the job book. The following table may be helpful in determining what weatherization measures are indicated from these comments.

Problem	Probable Cause	Remedy
Low house temperature High fuel use	High heat loss	Add insulation Add storm doors and windows Caulk and weatherstrip doors and windows
Cold floors	Cold crawl space or basement	Add banking to increase crawl space or basement temperature
Drafty house Results from convection currents	Loose doors and windows	Add storm doors and windows and caulk around windows and doors
Wet windows	Cold window surface or high humidity	Add storm windows or ventilate to reduce humidity
Wet walls or ceiling	Cold inside surface or high humidity	Ventilate to reduce humidity

3. *All windows should be fitted with storm windows.* Since this measure increases the insulation value of the window, as well as reduces the infiltration through windows, it usually results in the greatest benefit. Storm doors do not give as much benefit as storm windows. Weatherstripping exterior doors is nearly as effective as storm doors and not as expensive.

4. *Check to see if insulation can be applied.* If there is not at least 6 inches of insulation in the ceiling, 3½ inches in the sidewall, and 3½ inches under the floor, and if the basement or crawl space is unheated, consider adding insulation. It usually will result in a substantial heat saving. Check the job book to determine if insulation can be added to the areas where it is needed. It is usually easy to add insulation to an attic space and difficult to add insulation to a sheathed wall or below the floor.

5. *Check to see if the floor exposure factor (page 44 of the job book) and infiltration from the foundation (page 44 of the job book) can be improved by adding banking materials.* This procedure for adding banking materials is shown on pages 64-65 of the weatherization manual. If the floor is over an unheated area, consider insulating the floor; if over a crawl space, consider insulating the exposed foundation wall.

6. *Check to see if weatherstripping can be installed around single doors and windows or storm doors to reduce the infiltration rate.* Usually weatherstripping is not necessary if storm windows have been applied. This measure usually is not as effective in

reducing heat loss as those listed above, but if for any reason you cannot install storm doors and windows, make sure the weatherstripping is adequate.

7.   *Check to see if the infiltration through the wall can be reduced by caulking around doors and window frames.* This is one of the less effective measures of reducing heat loss; however, it may help in a loosely constructed building.

8.   *You now should be able to determine where the most logical areas for weatherization should occur.* Fill in the proposed changes in the third column of the summary sheet on page 49 of the job book, and calculate the heat saving from the proposed changes; use the procedure that was originally used in determining the heat requirements.

9.   *Check the availability and price of weatherization materials in your area.* Visit several building supply dealers, and determine what kind of weatherization materials are available and the price. It is a good idea to

make a list of these as you visit the dealer, and from these you will be able to select which dealer has the proper materials available at the most attractive price.

10. *Calculate the quantities of materials needed to complete the home weatherization,* page 49 of the job book.

11. *Complete the job sheet* on page 51 of the job book; list the materials required and their cost along with the instructions for applying the materials. This sheet is to go to the job site when the work is to be done, and any instructions required for the installation of the materials should be made on this sheet.

12. *Calculate the total cost of the weatherization materials* page 51 of the job book, and calculate the payoff time for weatherization materials.

Pages 30 through 40 of the manual shows examples of using the job book. Follow these pages carefully until you become familiar with the procedure.

Home Weatherization in Four Steps
Step 3: Evaluation of Data

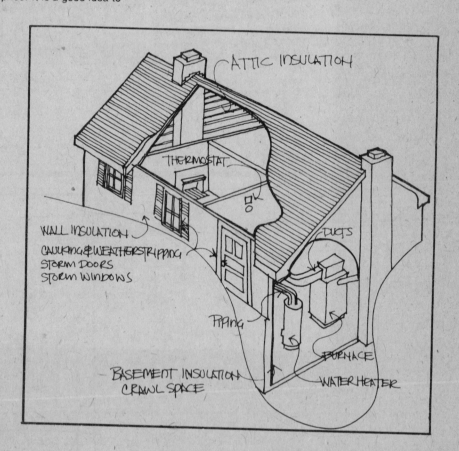

Example of Completed Job Book

Before proceeding to Step 4: Installation, the example of the completed job book (starting on the facing page) should be carefully reviewed until you are familiar with the procedure. Instructions for completing the job book are given on each page of the job book. Explanation of the procedure to be followed will be found in this manual on pages 26-29.

Home Weatherization Job Book for:

Name
MARY PERKINS

Address
3 PINE STREET
BANGOR, MAINE

SAMPLE 1

Description of Building

Sketch all views and put dimensions on each part shown, for example, length of walls, width and length of windows, etc. Label all single glass windows S and double glass and doors D. Complete all items in the job book labeled "Fill in at Job Site."

Front View

CAR PORT

6' 3' 5'
D 4' D S
8' 7'
33'

Left Side View

3' D 4'
8'
28'

Plan View

CAR PORT
33'
28'
24'
16'

Right Side View

THIS WALL INSIDE CARPORT — REGARD AS OUTSIDE WALL

3' 3'
D 7' S 4'
8'
28'

Rear View

DOOR TO CARPORT
6' 3' 3'
8' S 4' S 4' 8'
33'

Calculation of Floor Area

33	x	28	=	924
Building length ft.		Building width ft.		Floor area sq. ft.

FILL IN
AT JOB SITE

These grids are provided as guides for lines.
Drawings need not be done to scale.

Description of Building

Name of Head of Household
MARY PERKINS

Name and Address of Owner:
(if not the same as above)

Occupants of Structure:
5 Total number

Style of Structure:
☑ One-story
☐ Two-story
☐ 2-1/2 story
☐ Split-level
☐ Other (specify)

Age of Structure (approx.): 10 years

Rooms in Living Space:
6 Total number of rooms
6 Number used in winter

Occupants Comments (drafty, cold floors, too expensive to heat):
FUEL BILLS TOO HIGH
DRAFTY WINDOWS

FILL IN
AT JOB SITE

Heating System Information

Type of Fuel: (P = Primary) (S = Secondary)

☑ P Fuel oil
☐ Bottled gas
☐ Coal/coke
☐ Electricity
☐ Natural gas
☑ S Wood
☐ Kerosene
☐ Other (specify)

Type of Heating System: (P = Primary) (S = Secondary)

☑ P Steam/hot water/hot air
☑ S Fireplace/stove/portable heater
☐ Electrical baseboard
☐ Other (specify)

Domestic Hot Water:
Does central heating system provide heat for domestic hot water? NO

Thermostat Setting in Winter (average):
65° Day   60° Night   ____ None

Amount of Fuel Used Last Heating Season:

	Primary	Secondary
Type	FUEL OIL*	WOOD
Quantity	1500 GAL	1 CORD
Total Cost	$727.50	$75.00

District Heating Factor ____ 2

*48.5¢ PER GAL.

Heat Losses by Conduction Through Floors

R value of floor
List below all materials in floor deck, including carpet but not floor joists, starting from upper-most surface and working down.

Insert R value for each component from Table 1 (p. 23).

Material	Thickness (Inches)	R Value
Interior surface	–	0.68
LINOLEUM		.08
PLYWOOD	½	.65
SUBFLOOR	5/8	1.00
Interior surface	–	.68
	Total R value	3.1

Floor Exposure Factor
Select the appropriate factor from the descriptions below:

Building on posts or pillars with no skirts below floor	1.0
Crawl space skirted	.8
Rock wall basement	.8
More than 2 feet of base-ment wall exposed above grade	.8
Building on slab	.5
Building with tight crawl space	.5
Building with tight basement (heated or unheated)	.5

FILL IN AT JOB SITE

924	×	0.8	=	2
Floor area (from build-ing descrip-tion) sq.ft.		Floor Exposure Factor		District Heating Factor

2	+	3.1	=	477
District Heating Factor		Total R value		Heating Units Required

Potential Savings on Floor Heat Losses

Floors can sometimes be insulated to reduce heat loss but this is often difficult; where water pipes are below the floor, freezing problems may occur during very cold spells. However, every floor should be protected from drafts, so that it has a floor exposure factor of 0.5. With this exposure factor for this building, the heat loss through the floor would be:

924	×	0.5	=	2
Floor area from above. sq.ft.		Floor exposure factor		District heating factor

2	÷	3.1	=	299
District heating factor		R Value from above		Potential heating units

Subtract the potential heating units from those now required and enter here

Type of Heat Loss	Heating Units Required	Potential Heating Savings	Proposed Changes to Structure	Heating Units to be Saved
Conduction Through Floors	477	178	CAULK BASEMENT BANK WALL	

Heat Loss by Infiltration

On pages 31-33, calculate the heat loss by infiltration and by conduction through the separate parts of the building; enter the results in the table at the bottom of each page and in the summary table on page 34.

House Draft Index: Opposite each of the four component parts of a building in the table below, place a check mark in the circle adjacent to the features which best describe the condition of the building.

Building Component	One Air change per hour ①	Two Air change per hour ②	Three Air change per hour ③
Cellar or	Tight, no cracks, caulked sills, sealed cellar windows, no grade entrance leaks	Some foundation cracks, loose cellar windows, grade entrance not tight	Major foundation cracks, poor seal around grade entrance ✓
Crawl Space	Plywood floor, no trap door leaks, no leaks around water, sewer, and electrical openings	Tongue-and-groove board floor, reasonable fit on trap doors, around pipes ✓	Board floor, loose fit around pipes
Windows	Storm windows SOME with good fit ✓	No storm windows, good fit on regular windows	No storm windows, loose fit on regular windows
Doors	Good fit on storm doors	Loose storm doors, poor fit on inside door ✓	No storm doors, loose fit on inside door
Walls	Caulked windows and doors, building paper used under siding	Caulking in poor repair, building needs paint ✓	No indication of building paper, evident cracks around door and window frame ✓

Multiply the number of check marks in the first column by 1, the second column by 2, and the third column by 3. The Draft Index will be the sum of these products, divided by 4.

FILL IN AT JOB SITE

924	×	8	=	7392
Floor area sq.ft.		Height to ceil-ing (to upstairs ceiling in two-story house) ft.		Volume of air in building cu.ft.

7392	×	1.8	=	
Volume of air in building		Draft Index		

2	× .02 =	532
District heating factor		Heating units now required

Potential Savings by Reducing Infiltration

It should be possible to reduce the draft index for a building to 1 (that is, reduce the number of air changes to one per hour). If the draft index for this building were improved to 1, the infiltration loss would be:

7392	×	1	=	
Volume (from above)		Draft Index		

2	× .02 =	296
District heating factor		Potential heating units

Subtract the potential heating units from those now required and enter here

Type of Heat Loss	Heating Units Required	Potential Heating Savings	Proposed Changes to Structure	Heating Units to be Saved
Infiltration	532	236	CAULK & WEATHERSTRIP ALL WINDOWS & DOORS	

Heat Losses by Conduction Through Single-Glass Windows

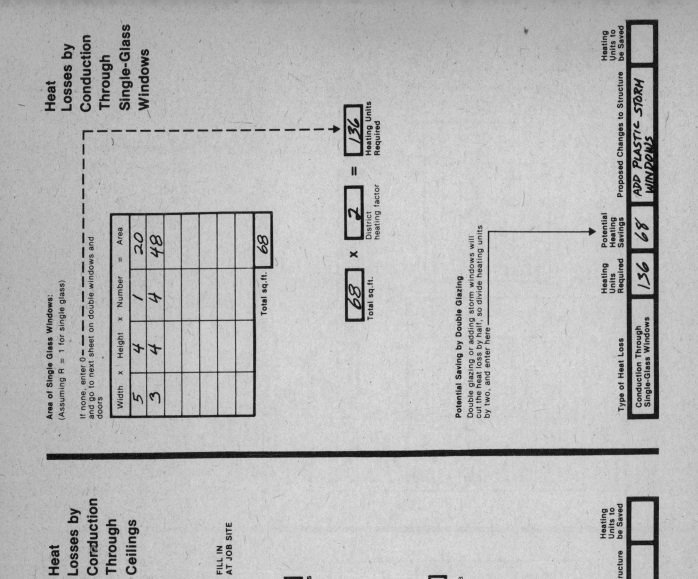

Area of Single Glass Windows:
(Assuming R = 1 for single glass)

If none, enter 0 and go to next sheet on double windows and doors

Width	×	Height	×	Number	=	Area
5		4		1		20
3		4		4		48
					Total sq.ft.	68

68 (Total sq.ft.) × 2 (District heating factor) = 136 Heating Units Required

Potential Saving by Double Glazing

Double glazing or adding storm windows will cut the heat loss by half, so divide heating units by two, and enter here

Type of Heat Loss	Heating Units Required	Potential Heating Savings	Proposed Changes to Structure	Heating Units to be Saved
Conduction Through Single-Glass Windows	136	68	ADD PLASTIC STORM WINDOWS	

Heat Losses by Conduction Through Ceilings

Area of Ceiling
(Take area of upstairs ceiling in a two-story house)

Ceiling area will normally be the same as floor area (from building description sheet)

Material	Thickness (inches)	R value
Inside surface		0.68
GYPSUM BOARD	3/8	.32
FIBER GLASS	2	7.40
Inside surface (0.68) OR	−	.68
Outside surface (0.17)	−	
	Total R value	9.1

12" Distance between joists/rafters:

FILL IN AT JOB SITE

924 (Ceiling area sq.ft.) × 2 (District heating factor) ÷ 9.1 (Total R value) = 203 Heating units required

Potential Savings by Insulation of Ceilings

A well-insulated ceiling (with 6 inches of insulation) should have an R value of 20. If the R value were 20 for this building, the ceiling heat loss would be:

924 (Ceiling area sq.ft.) × 2 (District heating factor) ÷ 20 (Total R value) = 93 Potential heating units

Subtract the potential heating units from those now required and enter here

Type of Heat Loss	Heating Units Required	Potential Heating Savings	Proposed Changes to Structure	Heating Units to be Saved
Conduction Through Ceilings	203	110	ADD INSULATION	

Heat Losses by Conduction Through Walls

Material	Thickness (Inches)	R Value
Interior surface	–	0.68
GYPSUM BOARD	3/8	.32
AIR SPACE	3/4	.91
FIBERGLASS	2	7.40
AIR SPACE	3/4	.91
SHEATHING	5/8	1.00
ASBESTOS SHINGLES	1/4	.13
Outside surface	–	.17
	Total R value	11.5

R Value of Outside Walls

List below all materials in walls, starting from inside and including air spaces within the wall. Insert R value for each component from Table 1 (see p. 23)

Note: Increasing thickness of asbestos shingles will actually reduce R-value. Asbestos shingles (1/8" thick) have .03 R-value.

FILL IN
AT JOB SITE

$$\boxed{122} \times \boxed{8} = \boxed{976}$$

Total perimeter of outside wall ft.   Total height of outside wall ft.   Gross wall area sq.ft

$$\boxed{976} - \boxed{158} = \boxed{818}$$

Gross wall area sq.ft   Total area of all windows and doors (from previous two pages) sq.ft.   Net wall area sq.ft.

$$\boxed{818} \times \boxed{2} \div \boxed{11.5} = \boxed{142}$$

Net wall area   District heating factor   Total R Value   Heating units required

Potential Savings by Insulation

Well-insulated walls should have an R value of 15. If this were so for this building, the wall heat loss would be:

$$\boxed{818} \times \boxed{2} \div \boxed{15} = \boxed{109}$$

Net wall area (from box above)   District heating factor   R Value   Potential heating units

Subtract the potential heating units from those now required and enter here

Type of Heat Loss	Heating Units Required	Potential Heating Savings	Proposed Changes to Structure	Heating Units to be Saved
Conduction Through Walls	142	39	NONE – WALLS CLOSED	

Heat Losses by Conduction Through Double-Glass or Plastic-Covered Windows and Through Doors

Area of Double Glass and Doors

(Assuming R = 2 for these units)

Width	×	Height	×	Number	=	Area
3		7		2		42
6		4		1		24
3		4		2		24
				Total sq.ft.		90

$$\boxed{90} \times \boxed{2} \div \boxed{2} = \boxed{90}$$

Total sq.ft.   District heating factor   R Value   Heating units required

Potential Savings

Triple glazing of windows can be done but is not usually practical. If no change were made in the windows, the potential saving would be 0 heating units and should be entered here

(If windows were triple glazed, the R value would be approximately 3, and the potential savings would be one-third of the "Heating Units Required.")

Type of Heat Loss	Heating Units Required	Potential Heating Savings	Proposed Changes to Structure	Heating Units to be Saved
Conduction through Doors & Double-Glass Windows	90	0	NONE	

Summary Table

Use the instructions provided in the Home Weatherization Manual to assess which potential savings can be obtained most successfully.

Fill out the following Summary Table by entering the "Heating Units Required" and the "Potential Heating Savings" from the corresponding tables at the bottom of pages 31-33. Then, write in the "Proposed Changes" and "Heating Units to be Saved" by such changes.

Heat Requirement Estimates (Annual Heating Units Needed)

Type of Heat Loss		Heating Units Required	Potential Heating Savings	Proposed Changes to Structure	Heating Units to be Saved
Infiltration	From Page 31	532	236	CAULK & WEATHERSTRIP ALL DOORS & WINDOWS	236
Conduction Through Floors	Page 31	477	178	CAULK BASEMENT BANK WALL	178
Conduction Through Ceilings	Page 32	203	110	ADD 4" INSULATION	110
Conduction Through Single-Glass Windows	Page 32	136	68	ADD PLASTIS STORM WINDOWS	68
Conduction Through Doors & Double-Glass Windows	Page 33	90	0	NONE	0
Conduction Through Walls	Page 33	142	39	NONE - WALLS CLOSED	0
Total		1580	631		592

Use the space below to calculate the quantities and cost of materials needed to make the proposed changes to the building.

INSULATION
CEILING — 924 SQ.FT. — ORDER 1000 sq. ft.

PLASTIC STORM WINDOWS — 5' WIDE PLASTIC
4 x 3 = 12
1 x 5 = 5
       17' — ORDER 20' + TAPE

BANKING — 4' WIDE PLASTIC: 33'+26'+35'=94'
ORDER 100' + TAPE

WEATHERSTRIP — 2 DOORS; 7x3' 17' EACH x 2 = 54 ORDER 35'

CAULK — AROUND 8 WINDOWS + 2 DOORS = 122' + BASEMENT
ORDER 6 TUBES

Job Sheet A

This Page
is Removable for
Use at Job Site

Name _____

Address _____

Type of Materials	Quantity Required	Estimated Cost	Location Where Materials Are To Be Installed (Walls, Ceiling, etc.)	Installation Figure No.	Special Instructions

(Insert Carbon Paper Under Table at Top of Page Only)

Map or directions for locating home:

FILL IN
AT JOB SITE

Technical Note on Savings: The percent in savings are theoretical and may be exaggerated under actual conditions. The indication in this example is that the homeowner will save a certain percent in each situation. This is highly unlikely. The homeowner will save only a percentage of the heat he is losing in one particular area. Each house is unique and a definite percent as a criterion is misleading.

Work record

Activity	Date	Supervisor	Comments
Order materials	10-5-77	E. HALL	ALL MATERIALS ORDERED
Install materials	10-28-77	S. PAUL	DOORS NOT WEATHERSTRIPPED

Home Weatherization Job Book for:

Name
William F. Laporte

Address
28 Haller Drive
Cedar Grove, N.J. 07009

SAMPLE 2

Description of Building

Sketch all views and put dimensions on each part shown, for example, length of walls, width and length of windows, etc. Label all single glass windows S and double glass and doors D. Complete all items in the job book labeled "Fill in at Job Site."

Right Side View

Front View

Rear View

Left Side View

Plan View

garage
24'
69'6"
31'
36'6"
18'6"
14'6
24'

Calculation of Floor Area

Building length ft	×	Building width ft	=	Floor area sq. ft
				2,611

First Floor:
24' x 14½' = 348 sq. ft.
31' x 36½' = 1,131.5 sq. ft.

Second Floor:
31' x 36½' = 1,131.5 sq. ft.
Total: = 2,611 sq. ft.

Garage:
24' x 18½' = 444 sq. ft.

FILL IN
AT JOB SITE

Job Sheet B

This page is Retained With Job Book as Permanent Record

Type of Materials Required	Quantity	Estimated Cost	Location Where Materials Are To Be Installed (Walls, Ceiling, etc.)	Installation Figure No.	Special Instructions
4" INSUL. 16" W/ V.B.	1000 sq. ft.	70.00	CEILING		TAKE SHEARS & STEPLADDER
POLYETHELENE 100 ft. 4 Mil. 4" WIDE		16.00	BANKING		
POLY 4MIL. 20 ft. 5' WIDE		4.00	WINDOWS		NEED KNIFE & STAPLER
MASKING TAPE 2" WIDE	3 ROLLS	6.00	BANKING & WINDOWS		
CAULKING COMPOUND	6 TUBES	6.00	WINDOW & DOOR FRAMES		NEED CAULKING GUN
WEATHER STRIP VINYL TUBING 35'		3.00	DOORS		NEED HAMMER
		Total Cost 105.00			

COST OF ONE HEATING UNIT:

1	×	.48	=	.48
Fuel Factor		Price of Fuel, per gal., cu. ft., KWH, cord		COST OF ONE HEATING UNIT:

Fuel Oil = 1
Electricity = 30
Natural gas = 120, Wood = 01

PAY-OFF TIME OF ONE WEATHERIZATION ACTIVITY:

This is the number of seasons for fuel savings to pay off the cost of this activity.

ACTIVITY: _Plastic on windows_

4.00	=	.37	good investment

Cost of activity (from job sheet above)

.68	×	.48	=	.06	"Pay-off" time (heating seasons)

Heating units saved (pg.32) | | Cost of one heating unit (from job sheet above)

excellent investment

PAY-OFF OF WEATHERIZATION

This is the number of seasons for fuel savings to pay off weatherization costs

105	=	.37	good investment

Total Cost (from job sheet above)

592	×	.48	=	

Total heating units saved (from pg.31) | | Cost of one heating unit (from job sheet above)

PAY-OFF TIME OF ONE WEATHERIZATION ACTIVITY:

This is the number of seasons for fuel savings to pay off the cost of this activity.

ACTIVITY: _add ceiling insulation_

70	=	1.3	good investment

Cost of activity (from job sheet above)

110	×	.48	=	"Pay-off" time (heating seasons)

Heating units saved (pg.32) | | Cost of one heating unit (from job sheet above)

These grids are provided as guides for lines
Drawings need not be done to scale

HEAT LOSS CALCULATION   35

Description of Building

Dwelling Unit Information

Name of Head of Household
William F. Laporte

Name and Address of Owner:
(if not the same as above)

Occupants of Structure:
[4] Total number

Style of Structure:
☐ One-story
[✓] Two-story
☐ 2-1/2 story
☐ Split-level
☐ Other (specify)

Age of Structure (approx.): 30 years

Rooms in Living Space:
[8] Total number of rooms
[8] Number used in winter

FILL IN AT JOB SITE

Occupants Comments (drafty, cold floors, too expensive to heat):
Drafty windows
High Fuel Bills

Heating System Information

Type of Fuel: (P = Primary) (S = Secondary)
[P] Fuel oil
☐ Bottled gas
☐ Coal/coke
☐ Electricity
☐ Natural gas
[S] Wood
☐ Kerosene
☐ Other ____ (specify)

Type of Heating System: (P = Primary) (S = Secondary)
[P] Steam / hot water / hot air
[S] Fireplace / stove / portable heater
☐ Electrical baseboard
☐ Other (specify)

Domestic Hot Water:
Does central heating system provide heat for domestic hot water? __yes__

Thermostat Setting in Winter (average):
65° Day   60° Night   ____ None

Amount of Fuel Used Last Heating Season:

	Primary	Secondary
Type	Fuel Oil	Wood
Quantity	3,500 gal.	2 cords
Total Cost	$1,680.00	$130.00

District Heating Factor ___1.25___
(see page 25)

Heat Loss by Infiltration

On pages 37-39 calculate the heat loss by infiltration and by conduction through the separate parts of the building; enter the results in the table at the bottom of each page and in the summary table.

House Draft Index: Opposite each of the four component parts of a building in the table below, place a check mark in the circle adjacent to the features which best describe the condition of the building.

Building Component	One Air change per hour ①	Two Air change per hour ②	Three Air change per hour ③
Cellar or Crawl Space	Tight, no cracks, caulked sills, sealed cellar windows, no grade entrance leaks	Some foundation cracks, loose cellar windows, grade entrance not tight	Major foundation cracks, poor seal around grade entrance
	Plywood floor, no trap door leaks, no leaks around water, sewer, and electrical openings	Tongue-and-groove board floor, reasonable fit on trap doors, around pipes ✓	Board floor, loose fit around pipes
Windows	Storm windows with good fit	Storm windows, good fit on regular windows	No storm windows, loose fit on regular windows ✓
Doors	Good fit on storm doors	Loose storm doors, poor fit on inside door	No storm doors, loose fit on inside door ✓
Walls	Caulked windows and doors, building paper used under siding	Caulking in poor repair, building needs paint	No indication of building paper, evident cracks around door and window frame ✓

FILL IN AT JOB SITE

Multiply the number of check marks in the first column by 1, the second column by 2, and the third column by 3. The Draft Index will be the sum of these products, divided by 4.

Draft Index:
$$2 \times 1 = 2$$
$$3 \times 3 = 9$$
$$\frac{11}{4} = 2.75$$

| 2611 Floor area sq.ft. | × | 8 Height to ceiling (to upstairs ceiling in two-story house) ft. | = | 20,888 Volume of air in building cu.ft. |

| 20,888 Volume of air in building | × | 2.75 Draft index | × | 1.25 District heating factor | x .02 = | 1436 Heating units required |

Potential Savings by Reducing Infiltration
It should be possible to reduce the draft index for a building to 1 (that is, reduce the number of air changes to one per hour). If the draft index for this building were improved to 1, the infiltration loss would be:

| 20,888 Volume (from above) | × | 1 Draft index | × | 1.25 District heating factor | x .02 = | 522 Potential heating units |

Subtract the potential heating units from those now required and enter here

Type of Heat Loss	Heating Units Required	Potential Heating Savings	Proposed Change to Structure	Heating Units to be Saved
Infiltration	1436	914	see note	☐

Caulk and weatherstrip windows + doors
Add storm windows + doors.

Heat Losses by Conduction Through Floors

R value of floor
List below all materials in floor deck, including carpet but not floor joists, starting from upper-most surface and working down.

Insert R value for each component from Table 1 (page 23).

Material	Thickness (inches)	R Value
Interior surface	–	0.68
Carpet + fiber pad		2.08
Hardwood floor		.71
Plywood	1/2"	.63
Interior surface	–	
	Total R value	4.78

Floor Exposure Factor
Select the appropriate factor from the descriptions below:

Building on posts or pillars with no skirts below floor	1.0
Crawl space skirted	.8
Rock wall basement	.8
More than 2 feet of basement wall exposed above grade	.8
Building on slab	.5
Building with tight crawl space	.5
Building with tight basement (heated or unheated)	.5 ✓

FILL IN AT JOB SITE

Calculation of Floor Area (First Floor: only):

24' x 14.5' = 348 sq.ft.
31' x 36.5 = 1,131.5 sq.ft.
_____
1,479.5 sq.ft.

1,479.5	x	0.5	÷	4.78	=	193.
Floor area (from building description) sq.ft.		Floor exposure factor		Total R value		Heating Units Required

Potential Savings on Floor Heat Losses
Floors can sometimes be insulated to reduce heat loss but this is often difficult; where water pipes are below the floor, freezing problems may occur during very cold spells. However, every floor should be protected from drafts, so that it has a floor exposure factor of 0.5. With this exposure factor for this building, the heat loss through the floor would be:

1,479.5	x	0.5	÷	4.78	=	193.
Floor area from above sq.ft.		Floor exposure factor		Total R value from above		Potential heating units

Subtract the potential heating units from those now required and enter here

Type of Heat Loss	Heating Units Required	Potential Heating Savings	Proposed Changes to Structure	Heating Units to be Saved
Conduction Through Floors	341	0	none	0

Heat Losses by Conduction Through Ceilings

Area of Ceiling
(Take area of upstairs ceiling in a two-story house)

Ceiling area will normally be the same as floor area (from building description sheet)

Material	Thickness (inches)	R Value
Inside surface	–	0.68
Gypsum board	3/8	.32
Fiberglass	2	7.40
Inside surface (0.68) OR	–	0.68
Outside surface (0.17)	–	
	Total R value	9.1

16"
Distance between joists/rafters:

FILL IN AT JOB SITE

36.5' x 31' = 1132 sq.ft.
14.5' x 24' = 348 sq.ft.
_____
1480 sq.ft.

1480	x	1.25	÷	9.1	=	203
Ceiling area sq.ft.		District heating factor		Total R value		Heating units required

Potential Savings by Insulation of Ceilings
A well-insulated ceiling (with 6 inches of insulation) should have an R value of 20. If the R value were 20 for this building, the ceiling heat loss would be:

1480	x	1.25	÷	20	=	93
Ceiling area sq.ft.		District heating factor		Total R value		Potential heating units

Subtract the potential heating units from those now required and enter here

Type of Heat Loss	Heating Units Required	Potential Heating Savings	Proposed Changes to Structure	Heating Units to be Saved
Conduction Through Ceilings	203	110	Add 4" fiberglass insulation	110

Heat Losses by Conduction Through Single-Glass Windows

Area of Single Glass Windows:
(Assuming R = 1 for single glass)

If none, enter 0 and go to next sheet on double windows and doors

Width	x	Height	x	Number	=	Area
3		4		14		168
6		7		1		42
5		4		2		40
2		3		2		12
				Total sq.ft.		262

262 (Total sq.ft.) $\times$ 1.25 (District heating factor) $=$ 328 (Heating units required)

Potential Saving by Double Glazing

Double glazing or adding storm windows will cut the heat loss by half, so divide heating units by two, and enter here

Type of Heat Loss	Heating Units Required	Potential Heating Savings	Proposed Changes to Structure	Heating Units to be Saved
Conduction Through Single-Glass Windows	328	164	Add Storm Windows	164

Heat Losses by Conduction Through Double-Glass or Plastic-Covered Windows and Through Doors

Area of Double Glass and Doors
(Assuming R = 2 for these units)

Width	x	Height	x	Number	=	Area	
3		7		2		42	(doors)
				Total sq.ft.		42	

42 (Total sq.ft.) $\times$ 1.25 (District heating factor) $\div$ 2 (R value) $=$ 26 (Heating units required)

Potential Savings

Triple glazing of windows can be done but is not usually practical. If no change were made in the windows, the potential saving would be 0 heating units and should be entered here

(If windows were triple glazed, the R value would be approximately 3, and the potential savings would be one-third of the "Heating Units Required.")

Type of Heat Loss	Heating Units Required	Potential Heating Savings	Proposed Changes to Structure	Heating Units to be Saved
Conduction through Doors & Double-Glass Windows	26	0		

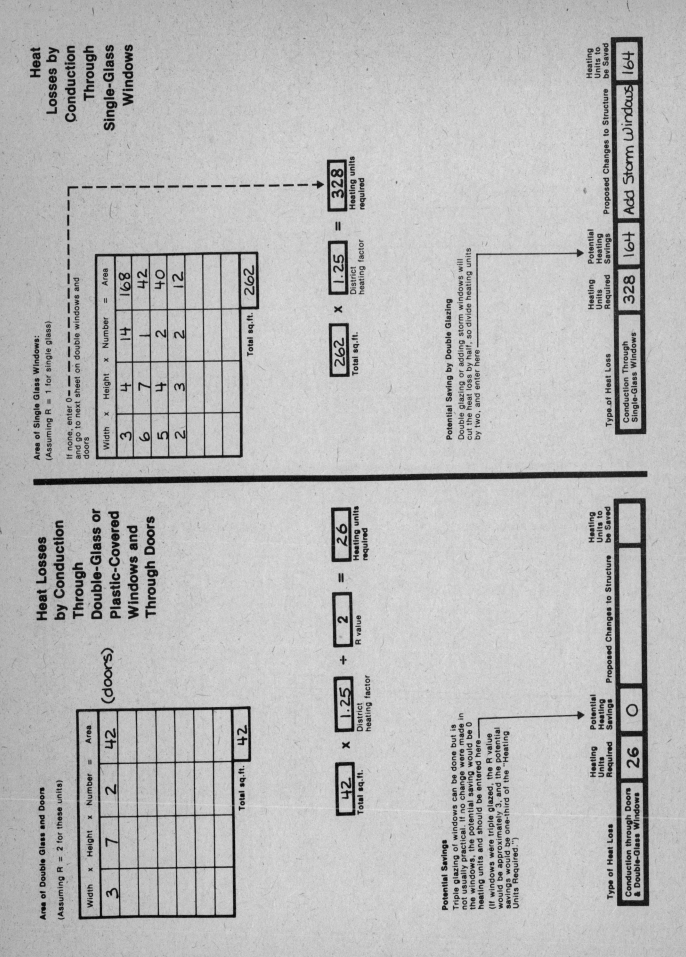

Storm windows and doors.

Use the instructions on page 40 of the Home Weatherization Manual to assess which potential savings can be obtained most successfully.

Fill out the following Summary Table by entering the "Heating Units Required" and the "Potential Heating Savings" from the corresponding tables at the bottom of pages 36-38. Then write in the Proposed Changes and "Heating Units to be Saved" by such changes.

Heat Requirement Estimates (Annual Heating Units Needed)

Type of Heat Loss		Heating Units Required	Potential Heating Savings	Proposed Changes to Structure	Heating Units to be Saved
Infiltration	From Page 36	1436	914	Caulk + weatherstrip windows + doors.	914
Conduction Through Floors	Page 37	341	0	none	0
Conduction Through Ceilings	Page 37	203	110	Add 4" fiberglass insulation	110
Conduction Through Single-Glass Windows	Page 38	328	164	Add storm windows	164
Conduction Through Doors & Double-Glass Windows	Page 38	26	0	none	0
Conduction Through Walls	Page 39	227	53		53
	Total	2,561	1,241		1,241

Use the space below to calculate the quantities and cost of materials needed to make the proposed changes to the building.

Caulking: (18 windows, 2 doors, 1 sliding glass door)
12 tubes

Ceiling Insulation (4")-16"
1500 sq. ft.

Storm Windows:
18

Storm Doors:
2

Wall Insulation:
Blown fiberglass, equivalent to 1"

Heat Losses by Conduction Through Walls

R Value of Outside Walls
List below all materials in walls, starting from inside and including air spaces within the wall. Insert R value for each component from Table 1.

Material	Thickness (inches)	R Value
Interior surface	-	0.68
Gypsum board	3/8	.32
Air space	3/4	.91
Fiberglass	2	7.40
air space	3/4	.91
Sheathing	5/8	1.00
Asbestos Shingles	1/4	.13
Outside surface	-	.17
Total R value		11.5

FILL IN AT JOB SITE

31' x 16' = 496 sq. ft.
36.5'x16' = 584 " "
36.5'x16' = 584 " "
14.5'x8' = 116 " "
7' x 8' = 112 " "
24 x16' = 384 " "
14.5'x8' = 116 " "
2,392 sq. ft.

Windows: 262 sq. ft.
Doors: 42 sq. ft.
304 sq. ft.

[ ] x [ ] = 2,392
Total perimeter of outside wall ft. | Total height of outside wall ft. | Gross wall area sq. ft.

2,392 − 304 = 2,088
Gross wall area sq. ft | Total area of all windows and doors (from previous two pages) sq. ft. | Net wall area sq. ft.

2,088 x 1.25 ÷ 11.5 = 227
Net wall area | District heating factor | Total R Value | Heating units required

Potential Savings by Insulation
Well-insulated walls should have an R value of 15. If this were so for this building, the wall heat loss would be:

2,088 x 1.25 ÷ 15 = 174
Net wall area (from box above) | District heating factor | R value | Potential heating units

Subtract the potential heating units from those now required and enter here

Type of Heat Loss	Heating Units Required	Potential Heating Savings	Proposed Changes to Structure	Heating Units to be Saved
Conduction Through Walls	227	53	Add Fiberglass Insulation (blown)	

Job Sheet A

Name: **William F. Laporte**   Address: **28 Haller Drive**

This Page is Removable for Use at Job Site

Type of Materials	Quantity Required	Estimated Cost	Location Where Materials Are To Be Installed (Walls, Ceiling, etc.)	Installation Figure No.	Special Instructions
caulking	6 tubes	9.00	windows + door frames		caulking gun
insulation 4", 16"	1,500 sq. ft.	187.50	ceiling		shears
insulation blown fiberglass		500.00	walls		contractor services
storm windows	18	630.00	windows		
storm doors	2	200.00	front + back doors		

(Insert Carbon Paper Under Table at Top of Page Only)

FILL IN AT JOB SITE

Map or directions for locating home:

Pompton Avenue to 28 Haller Drive, Cedar Grove

Work record

Activity	Date	Supervisor	Comments
Order materials	11-2-1977	B. Smith	work completed to
Install materials	11-2-1977	B. Smith	satisfaction of the owner

---

Job Sheet B

This page is Retained With Job Book as Permanent Record

Type of Materials	Quantity Required	Estimated Cost	Location Where Materials Are To Be Installed (Walls, Ceiling, etc.)	Installation Figure No.	Special Instructions
Caulking	6 tubes	9.00	Windows + door frames		caulking gun
4" insulation 1" equivalent blown insulation	1,500 sq. ft.	187.50	Ceiling		shears
		500.00	walls		contractor
storm windows	18	630.00			
storm doors	2	200.00	Front & Back		

Total Cost **1526.50**

COST OF ONE HEATING UNIT:

[1] x [.48] = [.48]   COST OF ONE HEATING UNIT:

Price of Fuel, per gal., cu. ft., KWH, cord

Fuel Factor
Fuel Oil = 1
Electricity = 30
Natural gas = 120, Wood = .01

PAY-OFF TIME OF ONE WEATHERIZATION ACTIVITY:
This is the number of seasons for fuel savings to pay off the cost of this activity.

ACTIVITY: _caulking and weatherstrip_

[9.00]   excellent investment
Cost of activity (from job sheet above)

[914] x [.48] = [.02]

Heating units saved (pg. 36) | Cost of one heating unit (from job sheet above) | "Pay-off" time (heating seasons)

PAY-OFF OF WEATHERIZATION
This is the number of seasons for fuel savings to pay off weatherization costs

[1526] Total Cost (from job sheet above)

[1241] x [.48]
Total heating units saved (from pg. 39) | Cost of one heating unit (from job sheet above)

= [2.6] "Pay-off" time (heating seasons)

PAY-OFF TIME OF ONE WEATHERIZATION ACTIVITY:
This is the number of seasons for fuel savings to pay off the cost of this activity.

ACTIVITY: _insulate walls_

[500] Cost of activity (from job sheet above)

[53] x [.48] = [20]   poor investment

Heating units saved (pg. 37) | Cost of one heating unit (from job sheet above) | "Pay-off" time (heating seasons)

Your Home Weatherization Job Book:

Name

_____

Address

_____

_____

Sketch all views and put dimensions on each part shown, for example, length of walls, width and length of windows, etc. Label all single glass windows S and double glass and doors D . Complete all items in the job book labeled "Fill in at Job Site."

Description of Building

Front View

Right Side View

Left Side View

Rear View

Plan View

These grids are provided as guides for lines. Drawings need not be done to scale.

Calculation of Floor Area

| Building length ft. | X | Building width ft. |

= Floor area sq.ft.

FILL IN AT JOB SITE

Description of Building

Dwelling Unit Information

Name of Head of Household

_____

Name and Address of Owner:
(if not the same as above)

_____

_____

_____

_____

Occupants of Structure:

☐ Total number

Style of Structure:

☐ One-story

☐ Two-story

☐ 2-1/2 story

☐ Split-level

☐ Other
  (specify) _____

Age of Structure (approx.):_____ years

Rooms in Living Space:

☐ Total number of rooms

☐ Number used in winter

Occupants Comments (drafty, cold floors, too expensive to heat):

_____

_____

_____

_____

_____

_____

FILL IN AT JOB SITE

Heating System Information

Type of Fuel: (P = Primary)
              (S = Secondary)

☐ Fuel oil

☐ Bottled gas

☐ Coal/coke

☐ Electricity

☐ Natural gas

☐ Wood

☐ Kerosene

☐ Other
  (specify) _____

Type of Heating System: (P = Primary)
                      (S = Secondary)

☐ Steam/hot water/hot air

☐ Fireplace/stove/portable heater

☐ Electrical baseboard

☐ Other (specify) _____

Domestic Hot Water:

Does central heating system provide heat for domestic hot water? _____

Thermostat Setting in Winter (average):

_____Day   _____Night   _____None

Amount of Fuel Used Last Heating Season:

	Primary	Secondary
Type	_____	_____
Quantity	_____	_____
Total Cost	$_____	$_____

District Heating Factor _____
(see page 25)

On pages 43-48, calculate the heat loss by infiltration and by conduction through the separate parts of the building; enter the results in he table at the bottom of each page and in the summary table on page 49.

House Draft Index: Opposite each of the four component parts of a building in the table below, place a check mark in the circle adjacent to the features which best describe the condition of the building.

Heat Loss by Infiltration

Building Component	One Air change per hour ①	Two Air change per hour ②	Three Air change per hour ③
Cellar or Crawl Space	Tight, no cracks, caulked sills, sealed cellar windows, no grade entrance leaks ◯ Plywood floor, no trap door leaks, no leaks around water, sewer, and electrical openings	Some foundation cracks, loose cellar windows, grade entrance not tight ◯ Tongue-and-groove board floor, reasonable fit on trap doors, around pipes	Major foundation cracks, poor seal around grade entrance ◯ Board floor, loose fit around pipes
Windows	Storm windows with good fit ◯	No storm windows, good fit on regular windows ◯	No storm windows, loose fit on regular windows ◯
Doors	Good fit on storm doors ◯	Loose storm doors, poor fit on inside door ◯	No storm doors, loose fit on inside door ◯
Walls	Caulked windows and doors, building paper used under siding ◯	Caulking in poor repair, building needs paint ◯	No indication of building paper, evident cracks around door and window frame ◯

FILL IN AT JOB SITE

Multiply the number of check marks in the first column by 1, the second column by 2, and the third column by 3. The Draft Index will be the sum of these products, divided by 4.

[ ] **X** [ ] **=** [ ]
Floor area sq.ft.   Height to ceiling (to upstairs ceiling in two-story house) ft.   Volume of air in building cu.ft.

[ ] **X** [ ] **X** [ ] **x.02 =** [ ]
Volume of air in building   Draft index   District heating factor   Heating units required

Potential Savings by Reducing Infiltration

It should be possible to reduce the draft index for a building to 1 (that is, reduce the number of air changes to one per hour). If the draft index for this building were improved to 1, the infiltration loss would be:

[ ] **X** [1] **X** [ ] **x.02 =** [ ]
Volume (from above)   Draft index   District heating factor   Potential heating units

Subtract the potential heating units from those now required and enter here ⟶

Type of Heat Loss	Heating Units Required	Potential Heating Savings	Proposed Changes to Structure	Heating Units to be Saved
Infiltration				

Heat Losses by Conduction Through Floors

Floor Exposure Factor
Select the appropriate factor from the descriptions below:

Building on posts or pillars with no skirts below floor	1.0
Crawl space skirted	.8
Rock wall basement	.8
More than 2 feet of basement wall exposed above grade	.8
Building on slab	.5
Building with tight crawl space	.5
Building with tight basement (heated or unheated)	.5

FILL IN AT JOB SITE

R value of floor
List below all materials in floor deck, including carpet but not floor joists, starting from uppermost surface and working down.

Insert R value for each component from Table 1

Material	Thickness (inches)	R Value
Interior surface	—	0.68
Interior surface	—	.68
	Total R value	

$$\boxed{} \times \boxed{} \times \boxed{} \div \boxed{} = \boxed{}$$

Floor area (from building description) sq.ft.   Floor exposure factor   District heating factor   Total R value   Heating Units Required

Potential Savings on Floor Heat Losses
Floors can sometimes be insulated to reduce heat loss but this is often difficult; where water pipes are below the floor, freezing problems may occur during very cold spells. However, every floor should be protected from drafts, so that it has a floor exposure factor of 0.5. With this exposure factor for this building, the heat loss through the floor would be:

$$\boxed{} \times \boxed{0.5} \times \boxed{} \div \boxed{} = \boxed{}$$

Floor area from above sq.ft.   Floor exposure factor   District heating factor   Total R value from above   Potential heating units

Subtract the potential heating units from those now required and enter here ⟶

Type of Heat Loss	Heating Units Required	Potential Heating Savings	Proposed Changes to Structure	Heating Units to be Saved
Conduction Through Floors				

Area of Ceiling
(Take area of upstairs ceiling in a two-story house)

Ceiling area will normally be the same as floor area (from building description sheet)

```
┌──────────┐
│          │
└──────────┘
```
Distance between joists/rafters:

Material	Thickness (inches)	R Value
Inside surface	—	0.68
Inside surface (0.68)	—	
— OR —		
Outside surface (0.17)	—	
Total R value		

FILL IN AT JOB SITE

```
┌──────────┐     ┌──────────┐     ┌──────────┐     ┌──────────┐
│          │  X  │          │  ÷  │          │  =  │          │
└──────────┘     └──────────┘     └──────────┘     └──────────┘
```
Ceiling area sq.ft.   District heating factor   Total R value   Heating units required

Potential Savings by Insulation of Ceilings
A well-insulated ceiling (with 6 inches of insulation) should have an R value of 20.
If the R value were 20 for this building, the ceiling heat loss would be:

```
┌──────────┐     ┌──────────┐     ┌──────────┐     ┌──────────┐
│          │  X  │          │  ÷  │    20    │  =  │          │
└──────────┘     └──────────┘     └──────────┘     └──────────┘
```
Ceiling area sq.ft.   District heating factor   Total R value   Potential heating units

Subtract the potential heating units from those now required and enter here ⌐

Type of Heat Loss	Heating Units Required	Potential Heating Savings	Proposed Changes to Structure	Heating Units to be Saved
Conduction Through Ceilings				

Heat Losses by Conduction Through Single-Glass Windows

Area of Single Glass Windows:
(Assuming R = 1 for single glass)

If none, enter 0 — — — — — — — — — — — — — — — — ┐
and go to next sheet on double windows and
doors

Width	x	Height	x	Number	=	Area

Total sq.ft. [____]

[____] **Total sq.ft.** X [____] **District heating factor** = [____] **Heating units required**

Potential Saving by Double Glazing

Double glazing or adding storm windows will
cut the heat loss by half, so divide heating units
by two, and enter here ────────────┐

Type of Heat Loss	Heating Units Required	Potential Heating Savings	Proposed Changes to Structure	Heating Units to be Saved
Conduction Through Single-Glass Windows				

Area of Double Glass and Doors

(Assuming R = 2 for these units)

Width	x	Height	x	Number	=	Area
				Total sq.ft.		

$$\boxed{} \times \boxed{} \div \boxed{2} = \boxed{}$$

Total sq.ft.   District heating factor   R value   Heating units required

Potential Savings

Triple glazing of windows can be done but is not usually practical. If no change were made in the windows, the potential saving would be 0 heating units and should be entered here

(If windows were triple glazed, the R value would be approximately 3, and the potential savings would be one-third of the "Heating Units Required.")

Type of Heat Loss	Heating Units Required	Potential Heating Savings	Proposed Changes to Structure	Heating Units to be Saved
Conduction through Doors & Double-Glass Windows				

Heat Losses by Conduction Through Walls

R Value of Outside Walls

List below all materials in walls, starting from inside and including air spaces within the wall. Insert R value for each component from Table 1.

Material	Thickness (Inches)	R Value
Interior surface	—	0.68
Outside surface	—	.17
	Total R value	

FILL IN AT JOB SITE

[ ] **X** [ ] **=** [ ]

Total perimeter of outside wall ft.   Total height of outside wall ft.   Gross wall area sq.ft

[ ] **−** [ ] **=** [ ]

Gross wall area sq.ft   Total area of **all** windows and doors (from previous two pages) sq.ft.   Net wall area sq.ft.

[ ] **X** [ ] **÷** [ ] **=** [ ]

Net wall area   District heating factor   Total R Value   Heating units required

Potential Savings by Insulation

Well-insulated walls should have an R value of 15. If this were so for this building, the wall heat loss would be:

[ ] **X** [ ] **÷** [15] **=** [ ]

Net wall area (from box above)   District heating factor   R value   Potential heating units

Subtract the potential heating units from those now required and enter here ⟶

Type of Heat Loss	Heating Units Required	Potential Heating Savings	Proposed Changes to Structure	Heating Units to be Saved
Conduction Through Walls				

Use the instructions on page 51 of the Home Weatherization Manual to assess which potential savings can be obtained most successfully.

Fill out the following Summary Table by entering the "Heating Units Required" and the "Potential Heating Savings" from the corresponding tables at the bottom of pages 43-48. Then, write in the "Proposed Changes" and "Heating Units to be Saved" by such changes.

Summary Table

Heat Requirement Estimates (Annual Heating Units Needed)

Type of Heat Loss		Heating Units Required	Potential Heating Savings	Proposed Changes to Structure	Heating Units to be Saved
Infiltration	From Page 43				
Conduction Through Floors	Page 44				
Conduction Through Ceilings	Page 45				
Conduction Through Single-Glass Windows	Page 46				
Conduction Through Doors & Double-Glass Windows	Page 47				
Conduction Through Walls	Page 48				
	Total				

Use the space below to calculate the quantities and cost of materials needed to make the proposed changes to the building.

Job Sheet A

This Page
Is Removable for
Use at Job Site

Name _____ Address _____

Type of Materials	Quantity Required	Estimated Cost	Location Where Materials Are To Be Installed (Walls, Ceiling, etc.)	Installation Figure No.	Special Instructions

(Insert Carbon Paper Under Table at Top of Page Only)

Map or directions for locating home:

FILL IN
AT JOB SITE

Work record

Activity	Date	Supervisor	Comments
Order materials	_____	_____	_____
Install materials	_____	_____	_____

Job Sheet B

This page is Retained With Job Book as Permanent Record

Type of Materials	Quantity Required	Estimated Cost	Location Where Materials Are To Be Installed (Walls, Ceiling, etc.)	Installation Figure No.	Special Instructions

Total Cost [ ]

COST OF ONE HEATING UNIT: [ ] X [ ] = [ ] **COST OF ONE HEATING UNIT:**

Fuel Factor
Fuel Oil = 1
Electricity = 30
Natural gas = 120, Wood = .01

Price of Fuel, per gal., cu. ft., KWH, cord

PAY-OFF TIME OF ONE WEATHERIZATION ACTIVITY:
This is the number of seasons for fuel savings to pay off the cost of this activity.

ACTIVITY: _____

PAY-OFF OF WEATHERIZATION
This is the number of seasons for fuel savings to pay off weatherization costs

[ ]
Cost of activity
(from job sheet above)
_____

[ ] X [ ] = [ ]
Heating units saved   Cost of one heating unit (from job sheet above)   "Pay-off" time (heating seasons)

$$\frac{\text{Total Cost (from job sheet above)}}{\text{[ ] X [ ]}} = \text{[ ]}$$

Total Cost
(from job sheet above)
_____

[ ] X [ ] = [ ]
Total heating units saved   Cost of one heating unit (from job sheet above)   "Pay-off" time (heating seasons)

PAY-OFF TIME OF ONE WEATHERIZATION ACTIVITY:
This is the number of seasons for fuel savings to pay off the cost of this activity.

ACTIVITY: _____

[ ]
Cost of activity
(from job sheet above)
_____

[ ] X [ ] = [ ]
Heating units saved   Cost of one heating unit (from job sheet above   "Pay-off" time (heating seasons)

51

PART 3:
SAVING COSTS OF HOME WEATHERIZATION

Home weatherization is a process which must play a large part in any serious effort on your part to conserve fuel. The heating and cooling of single-family homes is approximately 12% of the total United States energy supply. During colder than normal winters, like that of 1976-77, the percentage is even higher. Another important energy fact is that nearly 80% of these homes are inadequately insulated.

We live in homes so that we can protect ourselves from the elements, enjoy comfort and privacy with security for our family and our possessions. In the past, we have had to accept compromises, based on finances between initial cost and operating cost, size and comfort. Almost every home built in America has been constructed with insufficient insulation for today's energy costs and provides far from optimum comfort. Unfortunately, once built, a home cannot economically be completely renovated to achieve maximum economy, although improvements and even savings can be obtained by adding attic and crawl space insulation, storm doors and caulking windows, among other things.

The weatherization of your home (the process of making a home weather efficient in order to retain its heat in winter and to be cooler in the summer) is one of the wisest monetary investments you can make. Because of rising fuel prices, money invested in home weatherization will likely pay higher returns than investments in savings accounts, government bonds or in many cases, the stock market.

The government taxes income, including dividends from investments. But it doesn't tax the money you save in lower heating and cooling billings when you have "weatherized" your home. In addition, as one recent magazine article about solar heating pointed out, your "dividends" from conserving energy are largely recession-proof, inflation-poor, strike-proof and pollution-proof.

Besides helping you save money on fuel bills, weatherization increases the value and the saleability of your home. A home's fuel requirements are likely to become an increasingly important consideration for home buyers.

Most of the steps you take in winterizing your home will also reduce your summertime fuel consumption. A well-insulated home not only holds in heat during winter months, but does a better job of retaining coolness during the summertime. In other words, some of the investments in home "winterization" pay year-round dividends.

It is important to understand residential space heat in order to plan energy conservation measures. In the northern states, space heating forms a major portion (about 40% of the household energy) of the annual dollar budget for energy.

HOUSEHOLD ENERGY USE

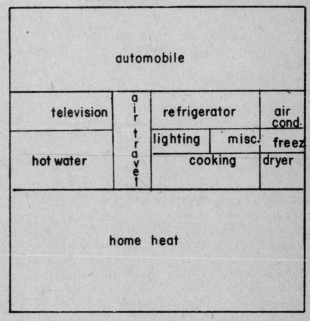

The estimated heat loss from an average residence runs about 100 x 10⁶ BTU/yr and costs about $750 annually to resupply at current fuel oil prices (1977). A rough picture of the distribution of heat loss in a typical home follows:

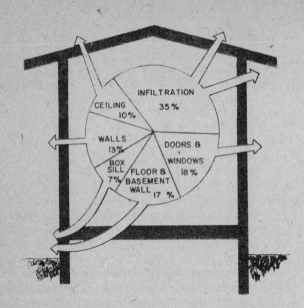

HEAT LOSS FROM A TYPICAL NEW HOUSE*

	Area	R Value	Notes
Walls	1,184 S.F.	13	3½" blanket insulation
Ceiling	1,680 S.F.	25	6" blanket insulation
Floor-Basement Wall	—	1.5	Concrete wall
Glass	220 S.F.	1.5	Double Glazing
Infiltration	13,440 C.F.	—	1 air change per hour

*Built to 1976 U.S. Department of Housing and Urban Development minimum property standards.

Retrofit Energy Conservation Techniques for Homes

This section presents a review of retrofit measures. Arranged as closely as practical in order of their probability return on investment, they are:

1. Energy management
2. Control of infiltration
3. Heating system maintenance and modification
4. Reduction of window loss
5. Addition of insulation.

All of the retrofit measures mentioned below are easily cost effective. Cost effectiveness is measured on a life cycle costing basis, and "average" or "typical" savings are just that. *It should be noted that savings measures are not always additive*; any savings from energy management and furnace modification should be subtracted from the heating bill and a new base created before savings from the other measures are applied. Note also that the *percentage of loss attributable to different areas will*

change as improvements are made. The following recommendations will often refer to a "typical house."

1. **Home Energy Management:** the term we are using for controlling the allocation of heat to a home both spatially and temporally offers the most energy (and therefore dollar) savings for the least investment of time, effort or money:

   a. **Permanent thermostat setback**—from 72°F to 68°F will save approximately 14% of a home's heating energy at no cost.

   b. **Nighttime Setback**—from 68°F to 55°F over eight hours offers an additional savings of approximately 13%.

   c. **Daytime setback**—from 68°F to 55°F over eight hours offers an additional savings of approximately 11%.

   d. **Zoned control** of heating is desirable, though somewhat difficult to accomplish in a retrofit situation. Some zoned control can be accomplished by adjusting valves or dampers to cut back heat to little-used rooms and hallways. Heat should be supplied to each room according to the normal activity patterns: kitchens often need less heat when the stove or oven is being used; dens and TV rooms need slightly higher temperatures to keep sedentary people comfortable. Savings depend on temperature reduction and floor area, but could be substantial.

2. **Infiltration** accounts for about 35% of heat loss in a typical home with reasonable insulation and may be as much as 75% in a home with *frequent, long* door openings and closings. This makes it the largest single factor in heat loss, but also the most difficult to predict because of differences in building orientation, position of windbreaks, construction quality, and door openings and closings. Any infiltration estimates then given for an "average" or "typical" house could vary by a factor of two—that is, they could easily be half or twice the amount predicted. Fortunately, the control of infiltration is a low cost item which is most appropriately done by the homeowners; thus, it is nearly always cost effective and most often results in substantial savings. Because drafts are a major source of discomfort, especially in homes where the thermostat has been set back, infiltration control is a necessary part of an overall conservation program.

   a. **Caulking,** when done by the homeowner, is an extremely low-cost measure with high returns if properly done. Attention to detail is important, and the best available materials should be used—i.e., acrylics, polysulfides, polyurethanes or silicones—even though their cost is two or three times that of cheaper materials. Heat loss due to infiltration through wall and

foundation openings may be 10 to 15% of total heat loss. If caulking could save even half of this, it would amount to 5 to 8% savings.

b. **Weatherstripping** also pays high returns, when done by the homeowner. Infiltration around windows and doors may account for 10 to 20% of total heat loss, with possibly half of this infiltration controllable by weatherstripping. The best available materials should be used, i.e., thin spring metal strips or rolled vinyl. Careful application is important.

c. **A vestibule**, which creates an air-lock door, is useful on a normal house and especially valuable if a number of children or pets are residents. Infiltration due to door openings ranges from 10% of heat loss in an average house to 45% of heat loss in a house with frequent long door openings and closings. Savings from a vestibule may be one-half of these figures.

d. **A windbreak** of closely spaced evergreens placed a distance of one to two house heights upwind from the dwelling may reduce infiltration 25 to 40% and heat loss by 10 to 15%.

3. **Home heating systems**, whether gas or oil fueled, are simple, sturdy and reliable devices which have changed little over the years. Recent fuel price increases, however, are sparking changes in the design of heating systems to increase their effectiveness. Some of these changes can be fitted to existing furnaces, and some must await a new furnace installation; some are available now, while others are still in the testing stage. The most promising are described below, though a local utility representative or building code inspector should be consulted before any changes are decided upon. And all work should be performed by a competent heating contractor.

a. **Annual maintenance** and frequent filter changes are necessary for safety and efficient energy use. They should be considered routine rather than energy saving measures.

b. **Duct work** is often leaky and should be checked and sealed in all areas.

b. **Ducts in unheated areas** should be covered with as much insulation as possible—up to six inches.

c. **An automatic damper** on the furnace flue or the use of *outside air* for combustion or a sealed combustion unit will save about 10% on an average heating bill. Sealed combustion has several advantages over an automatic damper; it is safer, quieter, and more effective because it does not allow the furnace to draw inside air for combus-

tion. Sealed combustion units will become more of a necessity as houses are sealed with weatherstripping and caulking. Neither system is easily available at present, though each can be obtained. Each should be available within a year and at a comparable price of about $100.

e. **Electronic ignition** systems for gas furnaces could save at least 5% of the energy used in heating. This will probably make them cost effective over a 10 to 20 year lifetime, though retrofit units are not readily available at present, and installed costs are difficult to estimate. Major furnace manufacturers should have electronic ignition systems available on new units within a year, and this will undoubtedly be cost effective.

f. **Re-sizing** of furnaces to produce more efficient operation has been shown to be very effective in many cases and should be considered, especially if heat loss is reduced.

g. **Other heating system improvements** such as primary heat exchangers, burners, fans, ducts and controls—even though they result in higher initial costs—are possible and should be examined and encouraged by state agencies and consumers. These improvements, taken as a whole, may make the installation of a complete new furnace a good investment.

h. **Safety**, in its many aspects, must not be overlooked in the quest for energy savings. Building inspection departments and utility service departments tend to put safety first in evaluating new products or modifications. This is a conservative approach and should be appreciated for what it is rather than as a conspiracy against energy conservation. As the number of "add-on" gadgets increases, safety will become more and more important and should always take precedence over supposed energy savings in determining product acceptability.

4. **Storm windows and thermopane windows** both come under the heading "double glazing" and should be considered. Triple glazing should also be considered. About 18% of heat loss occurs through windows and doors in a typical home with storm windows and triple glazing might save 10% or more on a heating bill. Heat loss due to windows is a combination of infiltration and conductive and radiative losses. The three components are somewhat difficult to sort out in a retrofit situation; therefore, savings from storm window addition will vary considerably.

a. **Double glazing** is calculated to cut heat loss through windows in half, increasing effective window R value from roughly 1 to 2.

b. **Triple glazing** can be accomplished by using inside storm windows over a thermopane window. According to most sources, these values are about 1, 1.5, and 2 for single, double, and triple glazing respectively.

c. **Additional window treatments** are desirable. Insulated shutters, drapes or shades can be made by the homeowners and provide good savings. Of these, shutters would be most effective. Since effective R value of a double glazed window is about 2 as compared to about 17 for a fully insulated stud wall, it is easy to see why a typical house with 15 to 20% window area loses so much heat through the windows.

5. **The addition of insulation** is a necessary part of any residential energy conservation program and tops the list for homes without any insulation. Since the knowledge and skill of contractors is quite varied, and since quality is difficult to assess or guarantee, a building owner should take time to ensure that he is getting a good job—concentrating on the measures above while doing this. Fire hazard and condensation are both potentially significant problems which should be considered.

a. **Attic insulation should be R22** 6-7" of fiber-glass batts, or better. The full thickness of insulation should be installed at one time to prevent recurring fixed costs of materials transport, etc. Annual savings in total heat loss may be 5% in a typical home with R-11 insulation and 20% or more in a home with no insulation.

b. **Stud walls** should be insulated to full thickness—R11 insulation or better. Annual savings in total heat loss may be 5 to 10% or more over an existing uninsulated wall.

c. **Masonry walls** should be insulated with a minimum of R7 insulation which may be applied outside or inside. Annual savings may be 5% or more, depending on the condition of the wall, amount exposed, and interior temperature.

d. **Floors** over areas such as crawl spaces or unheated areas should be insulated to R30 or the full depth of the floor joist. Annual savings may be 5% or more, depending on the temperature of the space under the floor. Special care must be taken for the pipes in the cellar area when insulating.

e. **Problems may arise with any insulation** job. Vapor barriers and ventilation must be properly installed to prevent moisture damage. Frost damage to basements and to water pipes is also possible. All these problems should be anticipated and examined. Once a home is properly weatherstripped and caulked (especially if a sealed combustion furnace is installed), interior humidity will probably remain at an acceptable level without the use of humidifiers. If used, power humidifiers should be carefully controlled to prevent excess moisture buildup which can ruin the effectiveness of insulation and damage wooden structures.

f. **Care should be taken in the choice and installation of materials** for any of the conservation measures listed above. As has been pointed out, the return on money invested in energy conservation is potentially large but is quite dependent on the quality of the work done. A building owner, therefore, should be advised to be prudent but not to "pinch pennies"—especially in materials, on a R per ft-basis, does not vary widely. Choices should be based on materials property and insulating value rather than on price.

Your Dividends Grow

You may not have thought about energy conservation this way, but investing in these improvements is better than most alternative low-risk, long-term investments you can make. When you invest in energy improvements, you immediately begin to earn dividends in the form of reduced utility bills. These dividends not only pay off your investment, but they pay "interest" as well. And, unlike dividends from many other investments, these are not subject to income taxes. At current fuel prices, the recommended improvements will pay for themselves many times over during the life of the house.

More important than the payback period are net savings. In a house, R-19 insulation in the attic would cost less and pay back faster than the recommended R-38. But the long run net savings are greater with R-38 because each additional resistance unit—up to the recommended level—pays back more than it costs. The best combinations shown in this booklet have varying payback periods, but they always yield the *greatest net savings* over the long run.

Even though utility bills rise as energy prices increase, the rise will be much less than it would have been without increased insulation. In fact, you might think of energy conservation improvements as a hedge against inflation. (Are you beating inflation with your after-tax dividends from other investments?)

Even if you don't plan to live in your house long enough to reap the full return on your investment in the form of lowered utility bills, it will probably still pay to invest in energy conservation improvements now. Because of higher energy prices, a well-insulated house is likely to sell more quickly and at a higher price than a poorly-insulated house that costs a lot to heat and cool. Show your low fuel bills to prospective buyers. They will find the small increase in monthly mortgage payments will be more than offset by monthly fuel bill savings, possibly bringing the cost of living in the house within their reach. The increased value of the house alone might cover the cost to you of making the investment in energy conservation improvements.

PART 4: A CLOSER LOOK AT YOUR HOME

Packages 1 & 2 (Natural Gas Heat)	Package 3 (Electric Air-conditioning)
Washington, D.C.	Washington, D.C.
Youngstown, Ohio	Cairo, Ill.
Shreveport, La.	Atlanta, Ga.
Eureka, Calif.	Oklahoma City, Okla.
	Bakersfield, Calif.

There are ranges of costs and saving given for the energy-saving home improvements below. Where your house falls in that range depends on the size and type of your house, the climate in your area, and what you pay for fuel. For purposes of comparison, a single-story, 1250-square-foot home in these cities will fall at about the midpoint of the range:

YOUR HEATING SAVINGS

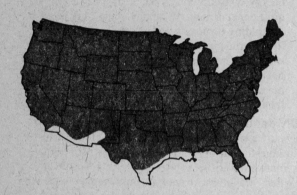

You can save significantly on heating if you live practically anywhere in the U.S.A.

Look at the map above.

If you live in the part of the country that's shaded, here are two packages of energy-saving measures for you:

Package 1 is cheap and easy, and it pays for itself every year.

Package 2 saves even more, year after year. It can cut your heating bills. It will pay for itself within 5 years.

Package 1

1. Turn thermostat down 6° in winter from your usual setting.

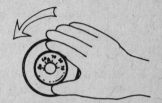

Package 2

1. Turn thermostat down 6° in winter from your usual setting.

3. Service your oil furnace.

IF YOU HAVE WHOLE-HOUSE AIR-CONDITIONING

Package 3

Here's the package of energy-saving measures for you.

Look at the map to the left.

Package 3 can save you money on your air-conditioning bills if you live in the shaded portion of the country.

2. Put on plastic storm windows.

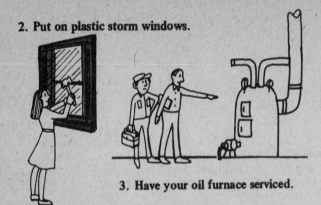

3. Have your oil furnace serviced.

Here's an idea of what **Package 1 costs and saves** in a typical home.

	Yearly Cost	Yearly Savings
1. turn down thermostat	$0	$20-65
2. put on plastic storms	$5-7	$20-55
3. service oil furnace	$25	$25-65
TOTAL	**$30-32**	**$65-185**

— If you already have storm windows, or if you don't have an oil furnace — then take a look at Package 2.

---

2. Put on plastic storm windows.

5. Insulate your attic.

4. Caulk and weatherstrip your doors and windows.

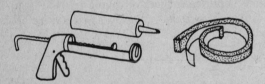

Here's an idea of what **Package 2 costs and saves** in a typical home (Items 4 and 5 reduce the heating bill to which the effects of Items 1, 2, and 3 are applied, so 1, 2, and 3 save less here than in Package 1):

	1st Year Cost	Yearly Savings
1. turn down thermostat	$0	$10-40
2. put on plastic storms	$5-7	$15-45
3. service oil furnace	$25	$15-40
4. caulk and weatherstrip	$75-105*	$30-75
5. insulate attic	$160-290*	$35-120
TOTAL	**$265-427**	**$105-320**

* These are do-it-yourself costs. If you called a contractor, these items could cost twice as much.

---

1. Turn thermostat up 6° in summer from your usual setting.

2. Insulate your attic.

3. Caulk and weatherstrip your doors and windows.

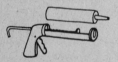

Here's an idea of what **Package 3 costs and saves** in a typical home:

	1st Year Cost	Yearly Savings
1. turn up thermostat	$0	$5-15
2. insulate attic	$160-290*	$25-50
3. caulk and weatherstrip	$75-105*	$20-50
TOTAL	**$235-395**	**$50-115**

* These are do-it-yourself costs. If you called a contractor, these items could cost twice as much.

You might or might not need to do all of these things. And if you live in the part of the country that's shaded on both maps, these cooling savings are *in addition* to what you save on heating.

Take a Quick

. . . . . look at your home from your armchair — you don't have to measure or count a thing. Depending on where you live and whether or not you have air conditioning, Part 3 will tell you what your best energy-saving steps are. You'll get a rough idea of what they'll cost, and how much they'll save you each year.

THEN ... DO IT!

. . . each energy-saving home improvement you've chosen is spelled out in detail. You'll find out how to do-it-yourself; or, how to hire a contractor and see that he does the job right.

There's More, too...

Part **6** has lots more ways to save energy — and some new ways to come in the future.

INSTALL STORM WINDOWS

PLASTIC

SINGLE-PANE GLASS

COMBINATION

There are three kinds of storm windows:

PLASTIC. These cost only 50¢ each. You may have to put up replacements each year.

SINGLE PANE GLASS. They cost about $10.00 each. You put them up and take them down each year.

TRIPLE-TRACK GLASS (COMBINATION). These have screens and you can open and close them. They are for double-hung windows only (like the one in the picture). They cost about $30.00 each installed. Double-track storm windows are also available, and they cost less.

All three kinds are about equally effective. The more expensive ones are more attractive and convenient.

CAULK AND WEATHERSTRIP YOUR DOORS AND WINDOWS

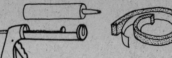

Caulking and weatherstripping are good cheap ways to save energy. It's worth your while to check to see if you need caulking, putty, or weatherstripping on your windows and doors.

DO THEY NEED CAULKING OR PUTTY?

Look at a typical window and a typical door. Look at the parts shown in the pictures. Check the box next to the description that best fits what you see:

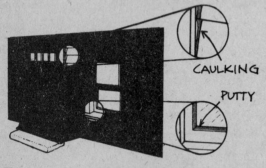

CAULKING

PUTTY

☐ OK ... All the cracks are completely filled with caulking. The putty around the window panes is solid and unbroken; no drafts.

☐ FAIR ... The caulking and putty are old and cracked, or missing in places; minor drafts.

☐ POOR ... There's no caulking at all. The putty is in poor condition; noticeable drafts.

If you checked either "FAIR" or "POOR", then you probably need caulking.

DO THEY NEED WEATHERSTRIPPING?

A. YOUR WINDOWS

Look at the parts shown in the pictures of one or two of your typical windows. Check one:

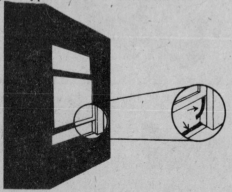

☐ OK ... Good, unbroken weatherstripping in all the indicated places; no drafts.

☐ FAIR ... Weatherstripping damaged or missing in places; minor drafts.

☐ POOR ... No weatherstripping at all; noticeable drafts.

If you checked either "FAIR" or "POOR", then your windows probably need weatherstripping.

B. YOUR DOORS

Look at the parts of your doors shown in the picture. Check one:

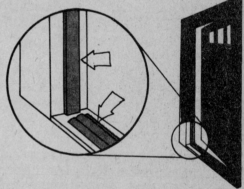

☐ OK ... Good, unbroken weatherstripping in all the indicated places; no drafts.

☐ FAIR ... Weatherstripping damaged or missing in places; minor drafts.

☐ POOR ... No weatherstripping at all; noticeable drafts.

If you checked either "FAIR" or "POOR", then your doors probably need weatherstripping.

INSULATING YOUR ATTIC

Attic insulation is one of the most important energy-saving home improvements you can make. This section talks about insulating 3 kinds of attics.

IF YOUR HOME HAS ONE OF THE 3 KINDS SHOWN BELOW,

go straight to the page in this section that applies, work it through.

Unfinished Attics

Unfinished Attic without a floor. (Attic isn't used at all—this includes Attics with roof trusses in them.)

Unfinished Attic with a floor. (Attic can be used for storage.)

Finished Attics

Finished Attic that can be used for living or storage.

IF YOUR HOME IS A COMBINATION OF TWO KINDS OF ATTICS

(part of your attic may be finished and heated, part may be unused except as storage, as in these sample houses):

If this is your situation, treat each of your attics separately

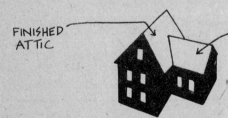

FINISHED ATTIC

UNFINISHED, UNFLOORED ATTIC

UNFINISHED, FLOORED ATTIC

Flat roof? Mansard roof?

If your home has a flat roof, or a mansard roof, it will be harder and more expensive to insulate than the others — talk to a contractor.

INSULATE YOUR UNFINISHED ATTIC

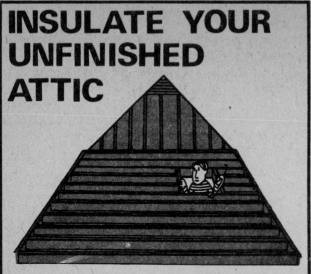

This is the kind of attic you have if it has no floor — at most some loose boards to walk on, and you don't ever plan to finish it.

Should you insulate it ?

It depends on how much insulation is already there. To find out, go up into your attic and measure the depth of the insulation.

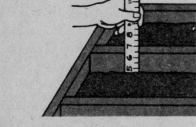

NO

If you already have 6" or more, you may have enough, and you can skip the rest of this page. Check the table on page 77 to be sure.

Yes

If you have less than 6", you may need more, and you should keep going on this page. Start by writing down the approximate thickness you have:

_____ inches

You'll need this number in a minute.

NOTE: If you can't get up into your attic to measure your insulation, you will need a contractor to do the work. Call him for a cost estimate. Ask the contractor to tell you how much insulation is already there along with an estimate for "R-19" insulation.

INSULATE YOUR UNFINISHED FLOORED ATTIC

This is your kind of attic if it's unfinished and unheated but has a floor.

Should you insulate it ?

It depends on how much insulation is already there. To find out, go up there and check.

The insulation, if there is any, will be in either of two places:

Between the rafters. The first place to look is up between the rafters and in the walls at the ends of the attic.

Under the floor. If it's not up between the rafters, it might be down under the floorboards. If so, it won't be easy to see. You'll have to look around the edges of the attic, or through any large cracks in the floor. A flashlight may be handy, and also a ruler or stick that you can poke through the cracks with. If there's any soft, fluffy material in there, that's insulation.

Wherever the insulation is, if it's there at all, estimate how thick it is.

No

If it's thicker than 4 inches, it's not economical to add more — skip the rest of this page.

Yes

If it's 4 inches thick or less, you might need more.

NOTE: If you can't tell whether you have enough insulation up there, get a contractor to find out for you. You're likely to be calling one anyway to do the work, and you'll want a cost estimate from him.

INSULATE YOUR FINISHED ATTIC

This attic is a little harder to insulate than an unfinished attic because some parts are hard to reach. A contractor can do a complete job, but if you do-it-yourself, there will probably be parts that you can't reach.

Should you insulate it?

You need to find out if there's enough insulation there already.

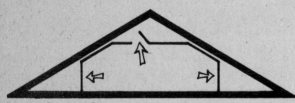

Depending on what your house is like, you may or may not be able to measure your insulation by getting into the unfinished spaces in your attic through a door or hatchway.

1. **IF YOU CAN GET IN,** measure the depth of insulation. If you have 6 inches or more of insulation everywhere, you have enough and you can skip the rest of this page.

2. **IF YOU CAN'T GET INTO THE UNFINISHED PARTS OF YOUR ATTIC AT ALL,** have a contractor measure the insulation for you. Ask him how much

When you go to take a look at these places, make a note of the depth of insulation that's already there; you'll want this information in a minute.

1. Which method?

You may have already found out that you can't do-it-yourself because you can't get into the unfinished part of your attic. If you can get in, there are some good things you can do yourself to insulate it.

Depending on your particular attic you may be able to do one or more of these:

A. INSULATE ATTIC CEILING

You can insulate your attic ceiling if there's a door to the space above the finished area. You should consider insulating it if there's less than 6 inches already there.

B. INSULATE OUTER ATTIC RAFTERS

"Outer attic rafters" are the parts of the roof shown in the picture below:

You should consider insulating them if:
- there's no insulation between the rafters; and
- there's room for more insulation in the outer attic floor and in the "knee walls" that separate the finished and unfinished parts of the attic.

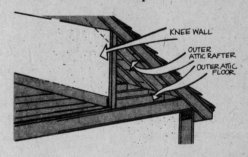

C. INSULATE OUTER ATTIC GABLES

"Outer attic gables" are the little triangular walls shown in the picture. You should insulate them if you insulate the outer attic rafters.

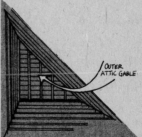

INSULATE YOUR WALLS

YOUR THERMOSTAT

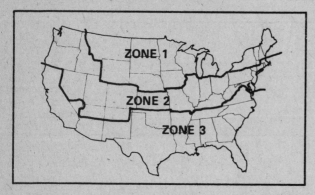

The table below tells you what percent of your heating bill you'll save by turning down your thermostat. Look at the map above to see which zone you live in. Read the column in the table for that zone. Circle either the top or bottom number in that column — you'll need it after you figure out your heating bill.

Circle the top number if you want to see what you'll save with a 5-degree turn-down from your usual setting.

Circle the bottom number if you want to see what you'll save with an 8-degree turn-down from your usual setting.

	ZONE 1	ZONE 2	ZONE 3
5° turn-down	14%	17%	25%
8° turn-down	19%	24%	35%

Table 1

2. Should you insulate them?

It depends on two things: the size of your energy bills and what your walls are like. To find out if you should insulate them, answer this question:

What are your walls like?

Most houses have *frame* walls. They have a wood structure — usually 2 by 4's — even though they may have brick or stone on the outside.

Some houses have brick or block *masonry* walls that form the structure of the house, without a wooden backup.

If you have frame walls, you should consider insulating them if there's no insulation at all in them already. A contractor can fill them with insulation and cut energy waste.

You may already know whether or not your walls have insulation in them. If you don't know, here's how to find out: Take the cover off a light switch on an outside wall. *(Turn off the power first.)* Shine a flashlight into the space between the switchbox and the wall material and see if you can see any insulation.

If you have masonry walls, it may be worthwhile to insulate them if they're uninsulated now, even though it's more complicated than insulating frame walls; call a contractor to find out what's involved.

Condensation in Walls

None of the insulating materials contractors blow into frame walls serves as a barrier to moisture vapor; condensation in insulated walls may be a problem:

Look at the map on page 58. If you live in Zone I, and plan to insulate your walls, you need to take steps to ensure that too much moisture from the air in your house won't get into your walls. (In Zone II the problem is much smaller.) If it does, it is likely to condense there in the winter, and you will run two risks: first, that your insulation will become wet and won't insulate; and second, that enough moisture will collect to cause rot in the structure. To help avoid these dangers, as a general rule, provide one square foot of ventilation for every 150 square feet of wall area. If you have adequate ventilation and moisture is not currently a problem you may:

1. Seal any opening in the inside walls that could afford a path to moisture, especially around the window and door frames.

2. Paint interior walls with a low-permeability paint; this can be a high-gloss enamel or other finish — ask your paint dealer.

INSULATING YOUR WALLS, FLOOR, OR BASEMENT WALLS

If you live in a climate where your heating bill is big enough to be a worry, it's a good idea to insulate the underside of your house. It won't save much on air conditioning, but it will save on heating.

The underside of your house looks like one of these.

A. A flat concrete slab sitting on the ground:

There's not much that you can easily do to insulate this type of foundation, and since it's hard to tell how much insulation is already there, it's hard to tell what your savings would be.

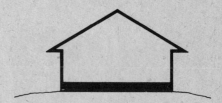

B. A floor over a garage, porch or open crawl space:

If there's an open space under your floor that you can't seal off tightly from the outside air, the place to insulate is in the floor, between the joists.

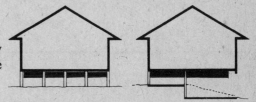

C. Walls of a heated basement that stick out of the ground:

If you have a basement that is heated and used as a living area, it may be worth your while to insulate the basement walls down to a depth of two feet below the ground.

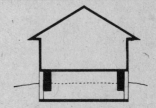

D. A combination of the above types:

Your house may be part heated basement and part crawl space, or some other combination. To estimate your costs and savings, treat each of the parts separately.

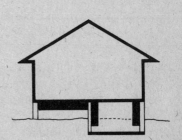

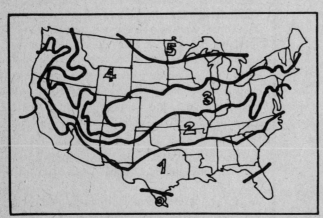

R-VALUE FOR:	ZONE 1	ZONE 2	ZONE 3	ZONE 4	ZONE 5
CEILINGS	R-26	R-26	R-30	R-33	R-38
WALLS	R-13	R-19	R-19	R-19	R-19
FLOORS	R-11	R-13	R-19	R-22	R-22

INSULATE YOUR FLOOR

There are two cases where it's good to insulate your floor:

1. You have a crawl space that you can't seal off in winter — for example, your house stands on piers:

2. You have a garage, porch, or other cold unheated space with heated rooms above it:

Should you insulate it?

1. Is your floor uninsulated?
2. Is the floor accessible?
   - If it's above a crawl space, is the crawl space high enough for a person to work in it?

SHOULD YOU INSULATE?

Exterior walls are the second largest area of the house where heat is lost. To insulate exterior walls of existing houses, insulation must be blown in. Insulating exterior walls can save 14 to 20% of the fuel bill.

To see if there is insulation in the walls, remove the plate cover from a convenience outlet on an exterior wall. If there is any insulation in the walls, it is generally not technically feasible nor economical to add more. If you did that, you not only would have the cost of the insulation but also the cost of repairing and restoring the holes in the exterior walls where it is blown in.

INSULATE YOUR BASEMENT WALLS

If you have a basement that you use as a living or work space and that has air outlets, radiators, or baseboard units to heat it, you may find that it will pay to add a layer of insulation to the inside of the wall. You only need to insulate the parts of the walls that are above the ground down to about two feet below the ground, as in the drawing above. Also, the cost figures given below allow for the cost of refinishing as well as insulating.

Should you insulate them?

Are your basement walls insulated? If they aren't, it pays to insulate them in almost any climate if you do the work yourself.

If you can't do it yourself and have to call a contractor, it will probably only pay to insulate these walls if your heating factor is bigger than 0.25.

PART 5: HOW TO DO IT

This part is divided into sections, each one treating an energy-saving step—
A section works like this:

First, how hard is it?

Should you do it yourself? – a quick rundown to help you decide whether you can handle it yourself or if you need the services of a professional.

Then, how to get it done

If you're doing it yourself:

    Tools you'll need   How much material
    Safety items to include   Getting it done, step by step
    What kind of materials

OR if you want to hire a contractor to do it, how to make sure he does the job right.

    What kind of materials   Signing a contract
    How much material   What to check
    R-Value

Last, more information you may need

Some general information that could be helpful:
    Buying Insulating Materials
    Choosing a Contractor
    Getting Financing

CAULK THE OPENINGS IN YOUR HOME

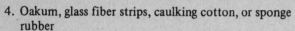

AN EASY DO-IT-YOURSELF PROJECT

Caulking should be applied wherever two different materials or parts of the house meet. It takes no specialized skill to apply and a minimum of tools.

Tools

1. Ladder
2. Caulking gun
3. Caulking cartridges
4. Oakum, glass fiber strips, caulking cotton, or sponge rubber
5. Putty knife or large screwdriver

Safety

You'll need to use a ladder to reach some of the areas which need to be caulked. Be sure you use it safely.

Level and block the ladder in place. Have a helper hold it if possible.

Don't try to reach that extra little bit — get down and move the ladder.

Carry your caulking gun with a sling so that you can use both hands climbing the ladder.

Materials

What you'll need

Caulking compound is available in these basic types:

1. Oil or resin base caulk; readily available and will bond to most surfaces — wood, masonry and metal; not very durable but lowest in first cost for this type of application.
2. Latex, butyl or polyvinyl based caulk; all readily available and will bond to most surfaces, more durable, but more expensive than oil or resin based caulk.
3. Elastomeric caulks; most durable and most expensive; includes silicones, polysulfides and polyurethanes; the instructions provided on the labels should be followed.
4. Filler; includes oakum , caulking cotton, sponge rubber, and glass fiber types; used to fill extra wide cracks or as a backup for elastomeric caulks.

CAUTION: Lead base caulk is not recommended because it is toxic. Many states prohibit its use.

Where a house needs to be caulked

1. Between window drip caps (tops of windows) and siding.
2. Between door drip caps and siding.
3. At joints between window frames and siding.
4. At joints between door frames and siding.
5. Between window sills and siding.
6. At corners formed by siding.
7. At sills where wood structure meets the foundation.
8. Outside water faucets, or other special breaks in the outside house surface.
9. Where pipes and wires penetrate the ceiling below an unheated attic.
10. Between porches and main body of the house.
11. Where chimney or masonry meets siding.
12. Where storm windows meet the window frame, except for drain holes at window sill.
13. And if you have a heated attic; where the wall meets the eave at the gable ends.

How much

Estimating the number of cartridges of caulking compound required is difficult since the number needed will vary greatly with the size of cracks to be filled. Rough estimates are:

        1/2 cartridge per window or door

        4 cartridges for the foundation sill

        2 cartridges for a two story chimney

If possible, it's best to start the job with a half-dozen cartridges and then purchase more as the job continues and you need them.

CAULKING COMPOUNDS

TYPE	RELATIVE COST	DURABILITY	COMMENTS
White lead-based	Least expensive.	1 to 2 years.	Allows for little expansion or compression.
Latex or butyl	Moderate.	5 years.	Can be painted.
Elastomeric Hypolon Polysulfide Silicon	Most expensive.	Indefinite.	Cannot be painted, but comes in colors.

Installation

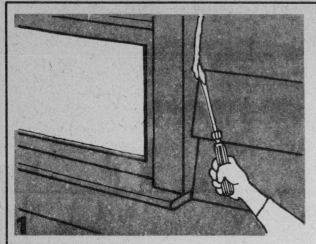

1

Before applying caulking compound, clean area of paint build-up, dirt, or deteriorated caulk with solvent and putty knife or large screwdriver.

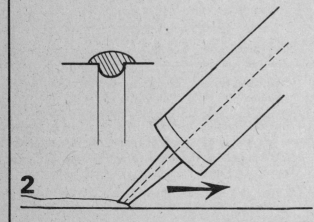

2

Drawing a good bead of caulk will take a little practice. First attempts may be a bit messy. Make sure the bead overlaps both sides for a tight seal.

3

A wide bead may be necessary to make sure caulk adheres to both sides.

4

Fill extra wide cracks like those at the sills (where the house meets the foundation) with oakum, glass fiber insulation strips, etc.)

FOUNDATION SILL

5

In places where you can't quite fill the gaps, finish the job with caulk.

6

Caulking compound also comes in rope form. Unwind it and force it into cracks with your fingers. You can fill extra long cracks easily this way.

WEATHERSTRIP YOUR WINDOWS

AN EASY DO-IT-YOURSELF PROJECT

Weatherstripping windows can be accomplished by even the inexperienced handyman. A minimum of tools and skills is required.

Tools

1. Hammer and nails
2. Screwdriver
3. Tin snips
4. Tape measure

Safety

Upper story windows may be a problem. You should be able to do all work from inside, but avoid awkward leaning out of windows when tacking weatherstripping into place. If you find you need to use a ladder observe the precautions on page 67.

Materials
What you'll need

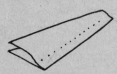

Thin spring metal

Installed in the channel of window so it is virtually invisible. Somewhat difficult to install. Very durable.

Rolled vinyl

With or without metal backing. Visible when installed. Easy to install. Durable.

Foam rubber with adhesive backing

Easy to install. Breaks down and wears rather quickly. Not as effective a sealer as metal strips or rolled vinyl.

Never use where friction occurs.

How much

Weatherstripping is purchased either by the running foot or in kit form for each window. In either case you'll have to make a list of your windows, and measure them to find the total length of weatherstripping you'll need. Measure the total distance around the edges of the moving parts of each window type you have, and complete the list below:

Type	Size	Quantity	X	length req'd	=	Total
1. Double-hung	1	(_____)	X	(_____)	=	_____
	2	(_____)	X	(_____)	=	_____
	3	(_____)	X	(_____)	=	_____
2. Casement	1	(_____)	X	(_____)	=	_____
	2	(_____)	X	(_____)	=	_____
	3	(_____)	X	(_____)	=	_____
3. Tilting	1	(_____)	X	(_____)	=	_____
	2	(_____)	X	(_____)	=	_____
	3	(_____)	X	(_____)	=	_____
4. Sliding pane	1	(_____)	X	(_____)	=	_____
	2	(_____)	X	(_____)	=	_____
	3	(_____)	X	(_____)	=	_____

Total length of weatherstripping required _____

Be sure to allow for waste. If you buy in kit form, be sure the kit is intended for your window type and size.

Installation

Thin spring metal

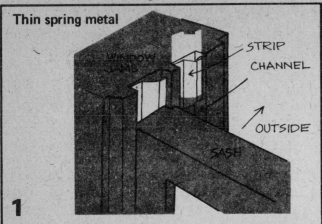

1

Install by moving sash to the open position and sliding strip in between the sash and the channel. Tack in place into the casing. Do not cover the pulleys in the upper channels.

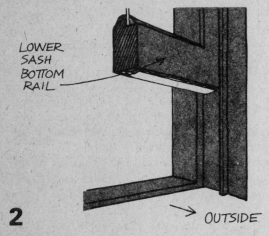

2

Install strips the full width of the sash on the bottom of the lower sash bottom rail and the top of the upper sash top rail.

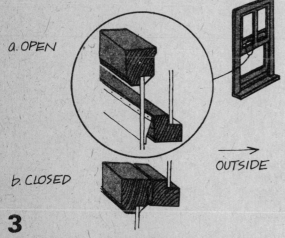

3

Then attach a strip the full width of the window to the upper sash bottom rail. Countersink the nails slightly so they won't catch on the lower sash top rail.

Rolled vinyl

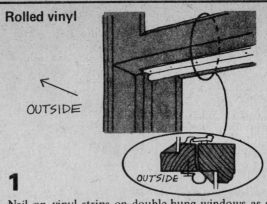

1

Nail on vinyl strips on double-hung windows as shown. A sliding window is much the same and can be treated as a double-hung window turned on its side. Casement and

2

tilting windows should be weatherstripped with the vinyl nailed to the window casing so that, as the window shuts, it compresses the roll.

Adhesive-backed foam strip

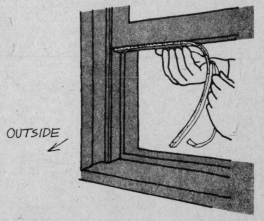

Install adhesive backed foam, on all types of windows, only where there is no friction. On double-hung windows, this is only on the bottom (as shown) and top rails. Other types of windows can use foam strips in many more places.

WEATHERSTRIP YOUR DOORS

AN EASY DO-IT-YOURSELF PROJECT

You can weatherstrip your doors even if you're not an experienced handyman. There are several types of weatherstripping for doors, each with its own level of effectiveness, durability and degree of installation difficulty. Select among the options given the one you feel is best for you. The installations are the same for the two sides and top of a door, with a different, more durable one for the threshold.

The Alternative Methods and Materials

1. Adhesive backed foam:

Tools

Knife or shears,
Tape measure

Evaluation — extremely easy to install, invisible when installed, not very durable, more effective on doors than windows.

Installation — stick foam to inside face of jamb.

2. Rolled vinyl with aluminum channel backing:

Tools

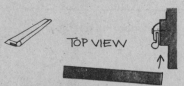

Hammer, nails,
Tin snips
Tape measure

Evaluation — easy to install, visible when installed, durable.

Installation — nail strip snugly against door on the casing

3. Foam rubber with wood backing:

Tools

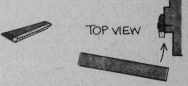

Hammer, nails,
Hand saw,
Tape measure

Evaluation — easy to install, visible when installed, not very durable.

Installation — nail strip snugly against the closed door. Space nails 8 to 12 inches apart.

4. Spring metal:

Tools

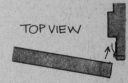

Tin snips
Hammer, nails,
Tape measure

Evaluation — easy to install, invisible when installed, extremely durable.

Installation — cut to length and tack in place. Lift outer edge of strip with screwdriver after tacking, for better seal.

Note: These methods are harder than 1 through 4.

5. Interlocking metal channels:

Tools

Hack saw,
Hammer, nails,
Tape measure

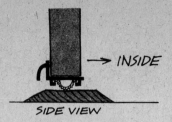

Evaluation — difficult to install (alignment is critical), visible when installed, durable but subject to damage, because they're exposed, excellent seal.

Installation — cut and fit strips to head of door first: male strip on door, female on head; then hinge side of door: male strip on jamb, female on door; finally lock side on door, female on jamb.

6. Fitted interlocking metal channels: (J-Strips)

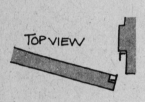

Evaluation — very difficult to install, exceptionally good weather seal, invisible when installed, not exposed to possible damage.

Installation — should be installed by a carpenter. Not appropriate for do-it-yourself installation unless done by an accomplished handyman.

7. Sweeps:

Tools

Screwdriver,
Hack saw,
Tape measure

Evaluation — useful for flat threshholds, may drag on carpet or rug.

Installation — cut sweep to fit 1/16 inch in from the edges of the door. Some sweeps are installed on the inside and some outside. Check instructions for your particular type.

8. Door Shoes:

Tools

Screwdriver,
Hack saw,
Plane,
Tape measure

Evaluation — useful with wooden threshhold that is not worn, very durable, difficult to install (must remove door).

Installation — remove door and trim required amount off bottom. Cut to door width. Install by sliding vinyl out and fasten with screws.

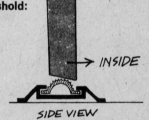

9. Vinyl bulb threshold:

Tools

Screwdriver,
Hack saw,
Plane,
Tape measure

Evaluation — useful where there is no threshhold or wooden one is worn out, difficult to install, vinyl will wear but replacements are available.

Installation — remove door and trim required amount off bottom. Bottom should have about 1/8" bevel to seal against vinyl. Be sure bevel is cut in right direction for opening.

10. Interlocking threshold:

Evaluation — very difficult to install, exceptionally good weather seal.

Installation — should be installed by a skilled carpenter.

INSTALL PLASTIC STORM WINDOWS

AN EASY DO-IT-YOURSELF PROJECT

Tack the plastic sheets over the outside of your windows or tape sheets over the inside instead of installing permanent type storm windows.

WINDOWS—THERMAL RESISTANCE

Single glass no storm window	R-0.88
Double glass window plus standard storm window	R-1.54
Triple glass window plus double glass storm window	R-2.13

Tools & Materials

1. Six-mil thick polyethylene plastic in rolls or kits
2. Shears to cut and trim plastic
3. 2" wide masking tape

   OR

3. Hammer and tacks
4. 1/4" X 1-1/4" wood slats

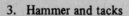

Installation

Measure the width of your larger windows to determine the width of the plastic rolls to buy. Measure the length of your windows to see how many linear feet and therefore how many rolls or the kit size you need to buy.

Attach to the inside or outside of the frame so that the plastic will block airflow that leaks around the moveable parts of the window. If you attach the plastic to the outside use the slats and tacks. If you attach it to the inside masking tape will work.

Inside installation is easier and will provide greater protection to the plastic. Outside installation is more difficult, especially on a 2 story house, and the plastic is more likely to be damaged by the elements.

Be sure to install tightly and securely, and remove all excess — besides looking better, this will make the plastic less susceptible to deterioration during the course of the winter.

INSTALL SINGLE PANE STORM WINDOWS

CONTRACTOR ASSEMBLY

DO-IT-YOURSELF INSTALLATION

Storm window suppliers will build single pane storm windows to your measurements that you then install yourself. Another method is to make your own with aluminum do-it-yourself materials available at most hardware stores.

Installation

Determine how you want the windows to sit in the frame. Your measurements will be the outside measurements of the storm window. Be as accurate as possible, then allow 1/8" along each edge for clearance. You'll be responsible for any errors in measurement, so do a good job.

When your windows are delivered, check the actual measurements carefully against your order.

Install the windows and fix in place with moveable clips so you can take them down every summer.

Advantages and Disadvantages

Single pane storm windows aren't as expensive as the double-track or triple-track combination windows (see page 75). The major disadvantage of the single pane windows is that you can't open them easily after they're installed.

Selection: Judging Quality

Frame finish: A mill finish (plain aluminum) will oxidize quickly and degrade appearance. Windows with an anodized or baked enamel finish look better.

Weatherstripping: The side of the aluminum frame which touches the window frame should have a permanently installed weather strip or gasket to seal the crack between the window and the single pane storm window frames.

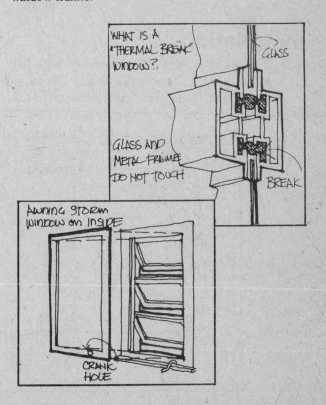

WHAT IS A "THERMAL BREAK" WINDOW?

GLASS

GLASS AND METAL FRAME DO NOT TOUCH

BREAK

AWNING STORM WINDOW ON INSIDE

CRANK HOLE

INSTALL COMBINATION STORM WINDOWS

CONTRACTOR INSTALLED

Triple track, combination (windows and screen) storm windows are designed for installation over double hung windows. They are permanently installed and can be opened any time with a screen slid into place for ventilation.

Double-track combination units are also available and they cost less. Both kinds are sold almost everywhere, and can be bought with or without the cost of installation.

NOTE: Most combination units will come with two or three 1/4" dia. holes (or other types of vents) drilled through the frame where it meets the window sill. This is to keep winter condensation from collecting on the sill and causing rot. Keep these holes clear, and drill them yourself if your combination units don't already have them.

Installation

You can save a few dollars (10% to 15% of the purchase price) by installing the windows yourself. But you'll need some tools: caulking gun, drill, and screw driver. In most cases it will be easier to have the supplier install your windows for you, although it will cost more.

The supplier will first measure all the windows where you want storm windows installed. It will take anywhere from several days to a few weeks to make up your order before the supplier returns to install them.

Installation should take less than one day, depending on how many windows are involved. Two very important items should be checked to make sure the installation is properly done.

Make sure that both the window sashes and screen sash move smoothly and seal tightly when closed after installation. Poor installation can cause misalignment.

Be sure there is a *tightly* caulked seal around the edge of the storm windows. Leaks can hurt the performance of storm windows a lot.

Selection: Judging Quality

Frame finish: A mill finish (plain aluminum) will oxidize, reducing ease of operation and degrading appearance. An anodized or baked enamel finish is better.

Corner joints: Quality of construction affects the strength and performance of storm windows. Corners are a good place to check construction. They should be strong and air tight. Normally overlapped corner joints are better than mitered. If you can see through the joints, they will leak air.

Sash tracks and weatherstripping: Storm windows are supposed to reduce air leakage around windows. The depth of the metal grooves (sash tracks) at the sides of the window and the weatherstripping quality makes a big difference in how well storm windows can do this. Compare several types before deciding.

Hardware quality: The quality of locks and catches has a direct effect on durability and is a good indicator of overall construction quality.

STORM WINDOWS		
TYPE	COST	COMMENTS
Wood frame, single panel glass.	More expensive.	Must be removed and stored in summer.
Aluminum frame, double glazed.	More expensive.	Must be removed and stored in summer. Double glass gives greater thermal resistance.
Aluminum frame with replacable screen.	Most expensive.	Comes with triple or double track. Can be left in place year round. Most durable, less breakage.
Aluminum frame, single pane glass.	Moderate cost.	Must be removed and stored in summer.

INSTALL COMBINATION STORM DOORS

NORMALLY CONTRACTOR INSTALLED

Combination (windows and screen) storm doors are designed for installation over exterior doors. They are sold almost everywhere, with or without the cost of installation.

DOORS—THERMAL RESISTANCE

1¾ inch exterior door.	R-2.04
1¾ inch exterior door and aluminum storm door (50 percent glass).	R-3.03
1¾ inch exterior door and wood storm door (50 percent glass).	R-3.70
Metal clad insulated door.	R-3.70

Installation

You can save a few dollars (10% to 15% of the purchase price) by installing doors yourself. But you'll need some tools: hammer, drill, screw driver, and weatherstripping. In most cases, it will be easier to have the supplier install your doors himself.

The supplier will first measure all the doors where you want storm doors installed. It will take anywhere from several days to a few weeks to make up your order before the supplier returns to install them. Installation should take less than one-half day.

Before the installer leaves, be sure the doors operate smoothly and close tightly. Check for cracks around the jamb and make sure the seal is as air-tight as possible. Also, remove and replace the exchangeable panels (window and screen) to make sure they fit properly and with a weather tight seal.

Selection: Judging Quality

Door finish: A mill finish (plain aluminum) will oxidize, reducing ease of operation and degrading appearance. An anodized or baked enamel finish is better.

Corner joints: Quality of construction affects the strength and effectiveness of storm doors. Corners are a good place to check construction. They should be strong and air tight. If you can see through the joints, they will leak air.

Weatherstripping: Storm doors are supposed to reduce air leakage around your doors. Weatherstripping quality makes a big difference in how well storm doors can do this. Compare several types before deciding.

Hardware quality: The quality of locks, hinges and catches should be evaluated since it can have a direct effect on durability and is a good indicator of overall construction quality.

Construction material: Storm doors of wood or steel can also be purchased within the same price range as the aluminum variety. They have the same quality differences and should be similarly evaluated. Aluminum and steel are good conductors and have greater durability than wood.

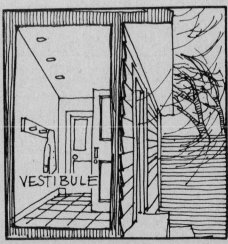

VESTIBULE

BUYING INSULATION

From the pages in Part 4 that deal with insulating your house you can get a good idea of what your choice of insulating materials is (see "Materials" at the beginning of each how-to section), how many square feet you need, and whether you need a vapor barrier with your insulation. There are three more things you need to know before you buy:

1. **What the R-Value of the insulation should be** — your money's worth in insulation is measured in R-Value. R-Value is a number that tells you how much resistance the insulation presents to heat flowing through it. This page lists recommended R-Values for the different parts of the house.

2. **What kind of insulation to buy** — pages 78 and 72 will help you choose the right kind of insulation for the job you want to do.

3. **How thick your insulation should be** — For the R-Value and type of insulation you're going to buy, look at the table at the bottom of page 79 — it'll tell you how many inches of each type of insulation it takes to achieve the R-Value you need.

---

1. What the R-Value of the insulation should be:

UNFINISHED ATTIC, NO FLOOR

Batts, blankets or loose fill in the floor between the joists:

Refer to tables on pages 23 and 79 for determining your present R-value.

THICKNESS OF EXISTING INSULATION	0"	to 2" or R-5	to 4" or R-11	to 6" or R-19	to 8" or R-26
HOW MUCH TO ADD	R-38	R-19	R-13	None	None
HOW MUCH TO ADD IF YOU HAVE ELECTRIC HEAT	R-38	R-26	R-19	R-11	None
HOW MUCH TO ADD IF YOU HAVE ELECTRIC HEAT & CENTRAL AIR CONDITIONING	R-38	R-33	R-26	R-19	R-11

Note:
1. If your home has no insulation, it is economical to add the full R-38 as indicated.

2. The "How Much To Add" recommendations inside the shaded area do not add up to the full R-38 recommended value due to 1978 costs of energy and insulation in "Pay-Off" time calculation (p.51). Any increase in energy cost should be recalculated for "Pay-Off" time.

FINISHED ATTIC

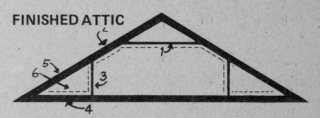

1. Attic Ceiling — see the table at the left under Unfinished Attic, No Floor.

2. Rafters — contractor fills completely with blow-in insulation; insulate only the areas noted.

3. Knee Walls — Insulate (5), Outer Attic Rafters instead.

4. Outer Attic Floors — Insulate (5), Outer Attic Rafters instead.

5. Outer Attic Rafters — Insulate areas *only* where adequate ventilation can be provided on the cold side of the insulation. In most situations, it would be better to insulate the "Outer Attic" floor and knee wall and provide ventilation for the "Outer Attic" space. Also, an airway between the insulation and underside of the roof should be provided in the sloped ceiling section.

6. End Walls — Add batts or blankets, R-11.

UNFINISHED ATTIC WITH FLOOR

A. Do-it-yourself or Contractor Installed:

Between the collar beams — follow the guidelines above in Unfinished Attic, No Floor.

Rafters and end walls — buy insulation thick enough to fill the space available (usually R-19 for the rafters and R-11 for the end walls).

B. Contractor Installed

Contractor blows loose-fill insulation under the floor. Fill this space completely — see page 77 for the R-Value you should get.

FRAME WALLS — contractor blows in insulation to fill the space inside the walls. See page 77 for the R-Value you should get.

CRAWL SPACE — R-11 batts or blankets against the wall and the edge of the floor.

FLOORS — R-11 batts or blankets between the floor joists, *foil-faced*.

BASEMENT WALLS — R-7 batts or blankets between wall studs. Note: Use R-11 if R-7 is not available.

2. What kind of insulation to buy:

BATTS— glass fiber, rock wool

Where they're used to insulate:
unfinished attic floor
unfinished attic rafters
underside of floors

best suited for standard joist or rafter spacing of 16" or 24", and space between joists relatively free of obstructions

cut in sections 15" or 23" wide, 1" to 7" thick, 4' or 8' long

with or without a vapor barrier backing — if you need one and can't get it, buy polyethylene except that to be used to insulate the underside of floors

easy to handle because of relatively small size

use will result in more waste from trimming sections than use of blankets

fire resistant, moisture resistant

FOAMED IN PLACE— ureaformaldahyde

CHECK STATE AND LOCAL FIRE CODES.

moisture resistant, fire resistant

may have higher insulating value than blown-in materials

more expensive than blown-in materials

quality of application to date has been very inconsistent — choose a qualified contractor who will guarantee his work.

BLANKETS— glass fiber, rock wool

Where they're used to insulate:
unfinished attic floor
unfinished attic rafters
underside of floors

best suited for standard joist or rafter spacing of 16" or 24", and space between joists relatively free of obstructions

cut in sections 15" or 23" wide, 1" to 7" thick in rolls to be cut to length by the installer

with or without a vapor barrier backing

a little more difficult to handle than batts because of size

fire resistant, moisture resistant

RIGID BOARD— extruded polystyrene bead board (expanded polystyrene) urethane board, glass fiber

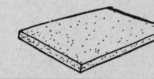

Where it's used to insulate:
basement wall

NOTE: Polystyrene and urethane rigid board insulation should only be installed by a contractor. They must be covered with 1/2" gypsum wallboard to assure fire safety.

extruded polystyrene and urethane are their own vapor barriers, bead board and glass fiber are not.

high insulating value for relatively small thicknesses, particularly urethane.

comes in 24" or 48" widths

variety of thicknesses from 3/4" to 4"

LOOSE FILL (poured-in) — glass fiber, rock wool, cellulosic fiber, vermiculite, perlite

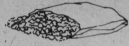

Where it's used to insulate:

unfinished attic floor

vapor barrier bought and applied separately

best suited for non-standard or irregular joist spacing or when space between joists has many obstructions

glass fiber and rock wool are fire resistant and moisture resistant

cellulosic fiber chemically treated to be fire resistant and moisture resistant; treatment not yet proven to be heat resistant, may break down in a hot attic; check to be sure that bags indicate material meets Federal Specifications. If they do, they'll be clearly labelled.

vermiculite is significantly more expensive but can be poured into smaller areas.

vermiculite and perlite have about the same insulating value.

all are easy to install.

LOOSE FILL (blown-in) — glass fiber, rock wool, cellulosic fiber

Where it's used to insulate

unfinished attic floor

finished attic floor

finished frame walls

underside of floors

vapor barrier bought separately

same physical properties as poured-in loose fill.

Because it consists of smaller tufts, cellulosic fiber gets into small nooks and corners more consistently than rock wool or glass fiber when blown into closed spaces such as walls or joist spaces.

When any of these materials are blown into a closed space enough must be blown in to fill the whole space.

3. How thick your insulation should be:

Get the R-Value you need from page 77, and the type of insulation you need from this page and the one before. Use the table below to find out how thick the insulation you buy should be:

TYPE OF INSULATION

	BATTS OR BLANKETS		LOOSE FILL (POURED-IN)			
	glass fiber	rock wool	glass fiber	rock wool	cellulosic fiber	
R-11	3½"-4"	3"	5"	4"	3"	R-11
R-19	6"-6½"	5¼"	8"-9"	6"-7"	5"	R-19
R-22	6½"	6"	10"	7"-8"	6"	R-22
R-30	9½"-10½"*	9"*	13"-14"	10"-11"	8"	R-30
R-38	12"-13"*	10½"*	17"-18"	13"-14"	10"-11"	R-38

* two batts or blankets required.

INSULATE YOUR UNFINISHED ATTIC

AN EASY DO-IT-YOURSELF PROJECT

Install batts or blankets between the joists or trusses in your attic

OR

Pour in loose fill between the joists or trusses

OR

Lay in batts or pour in loose fill over existing insulation if you've decided you don't have enough already. *Don't* add a vapor barrier if you're installing additional insulation.

NOTE: If your attic has trusses in it, this section still applies — the insulation goes in the same place, but job is more difficult.

Tools

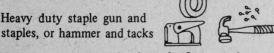

1. Temporary lighting

2. Temporary flooring

3. Duct or masking tape (2" wide)

4. Heavy duty staple gun and staples, or hammer and tacks

5. Heavy duty shears or linoleum knife to cut batts or blankets and plastic for vapor barrier

Safety

1. Provide good lighting

2. Lay boards or plywood sheets down over the tops of the joists or trusses to form a walkway (the ceiling below won't support your weight).

3. Be careful of roofing nails protruding through roof sheathing.

4. If you use glass fiber or mineral wool, wear gloves and breathing mask, and keep the material wrapped until you're ready to put it in place.

5. When working with any glass fiber or rock wool insulation, wear gloves, breathing mask, *and* goggles to avoid injury.

Materials
What you'll need

Batts, glass fiber or rock wool

Blankets, glass fiber or rock wool

Loose fill, rock wool, cellulosic fiber, or vermiculite

Vapor barriers

How much

(a) Accurately determine your attic area.

If necessary, divide it into rectangles and sum the areas.

____ X ____ = ____
____ X ____ = ____
____ X ____ = ____
Total = ____

(b) Insulation area = (.9) X (total) = ____

(c) Vapor barrier area (see if you need one — page 87).

  1. Batts or blankets with vapor barrier backing — use insulation area.

  2. Polyethylene (for use with loose fill, or if backed batts or blankets are not available) — use insulation area, but plan on waste since the polyethylene will be installed in strips between the joists or trusses, and you may not be able to cut an even number of strips out of a roll.

(d) Insulation thickness — see page 79. If page 77 calls for R-30 or more, you may be adding two layers of insulation. Lay the first layer between the joists, and the second layer across the joists. (This is very difficult with trusses — lay the second layer parallel to the trusses, or even better, — use loose fill.) Figure attic area for the second layer.

Installation

Preparation

Put in temporary lighting and flooring, check for leaks and check need for ventilation and vapor barrier (see page 87). Seal all places where pipes or wires penetrate the attic floor. **NOTE:** Some manufacturers may recommend using polyethylene in a continuous sheet across the joists or trusses. If you aren't adding insulation that covers the tops of these framing members with at least 3½" of insulation, laying a continuous sheet may cause condensation along them; lay strips as shown instead.

1

Install temporary flooring and lights. Keep insulation in wrappers until you are ready to install. It comes wrapped in a compressed state and expands when the wrappers are removed.

3

Install separate vapor barrier if needed (see page 87). Lay in polyethylene strips between joists or trusses. Staple or tack in place. Seal seams and holes with tape. (Seams may be overlapped 6" instead.)

2

Check for roof leaks, looking for water stains or marks. If you find leakage, make repairs before you insulate. Wet insulation is ineffective and can damage the structure of your home.

4

If you're using loose fill, install baffles at the inside of the eave vents so that the insulation won't block the flow of air from the vents into the attic. Be sure that insulation extends out far enough to cover the top plate.

Installing the insulation

Either lay in batts or blankets between the joists or pour in loose fill. If you're using batts or blankets with a vapor barrier, place the barrier on the side toward the living area.

5

Lay in blankets or batts between joists or trusses. (Note: batts and blankets are slightly wider than joist spacing so they'll fit snugly). If blankets are used, cut long runs first to conserve material, using leftovers for shorter spaces. Slide insulation under wiring wherever possible.

7

The space between the chimney and the wood framing should be filled with *non-combustible* material, preferably unfaced batts or blankets. Also, the National Electric Code requires that insulation be kept 3" away from light fixtures.

OR

6

Pour in loose fill insulation between the joists up to the top of the joists. Use a board or garden rake to level it. Fill all the nooks and crannies but don't cover recessed light fixtures or exhaust fans.

8

Cut ends of batts or blankets to fit snugly around cross bracing. Cut the next batt in a similar way to allow the ends to butt tightly together. If page 77 calls for an R-Value that requires a second layer, place it **at right angles** to the joists.

INSULATE YOUR UNFINISHED FLOORED ATTIC

TWO OPTIONS AVAILABLE

1. **CONTRACTOR INSTALLED:** blow-in insulation under the flooring and between the joists.
2. **DO IT YOURSELF OR CONTRACTOR:** install batts between the rafters, collar beams, and the studs on the end walls.

CONTRACTOR INSTALLED

Types of materials contractors use

Blown-in insulation
   glass fiber
   rock wool
   cellulosic fiber

Preparation

Do you need ventilation in your attic? See page 87.

Check for roof leaks, looking for water stains or marks. If you can find any leaks, make repairs before you insulate. Wet insulation is useless and can damage the structure of your house.

What your contractor will do

The insulation is installed by blowing the insulating material under air pressure through a big flexible hose into the spaces between the attic floor and the ceiling of the rooms below. Bags of insulating material are fed into a blowing machine that mixes the insulation with air and forces it through the hose and into place. Before starting

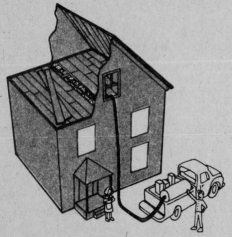

the machine, the contractor will locate the cross bracing between the joists in the attic. He'll then remove the floor boards above the cross bracing and install the insulation by blowing it in on each side of the cross bracing to make sure there are no spaces left unfilled. Since there's no effective way to partially fill a space, all of the spaces should be completely filled to ensure proper coverage. Normally the job will take no longer than a day.

What you should check

First be very careful about choosing a contractor.

Before you sign an agreement with your contractor, decide how much and what kind of insulation you're buying and make sure it's included in the contract. Insulation material properly installed will achieve a single insulating value (R-Value) for the depth of your joist space. You should agree on what that insulating value is with the contractor, before the job begins. Next check a bag of the type of insulation he intends to use. On it, there will be a table which will indicate how many square feet of attic floor that bag is meant to cover while achieving the desired insulating value. The information may be in different forms (number of square feet per bag or number of bags per 1000 square feet), so you may have to do some simple division to use the number correctly. Knowing this and the area of your attic, you should be able to figure out how many bags must be installed to give you the desired R-Value. This number should be agreed upon between you and the contractor before the job is begun. While the job is in progress, be sure the right amount is being installed. There's nothing wrong with having the contractor save the empty bags so that you can count them (5 bags more or less than the amount you agreed on is an acceptable difference from the estimate).

After the job is finished, it's a good idea to drill 1/4" diameter holes in the floor about a foot apart. This will help prevent condensation from collecting under the floor in winter.

DO-IT-YOURSELF

Install batts or blankets in your attic between the rafters and collar beams, and the studs on the end walls.

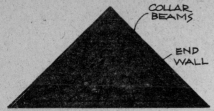

This measure will involve installing 2x4 beams which span between each roof rafter at ceiling height, if your attic doesn't already have them. This gives you a ventilation space above for the insulation (see page 87).

NOTE: The materials, methods, and thicknesses of insulation are the same for both do-it-yourself and contractor jobs.

Safety

1. Provide good lighting
2. Be careful of roofing nails protruding through the roof sheathing
3. If you use glass fiber or mineral wool, wear gloves and a breathing mask and keep the material wrapped until you're about to use it

Tools

1. Temporary lighting
2. Heavy duty staple gun and staples
3. Linoleum knife or heavy duty shears to cut the insulation
4. Duct or masking tape (2" wide)
5. Hammer, nails (only if you're putting in collar beams)
6. Power or hand saw (only if you're putting in collar beams)

Materials

What you'll need

Buy either batts or blankets, made out of glass fiber or rock wool.

Do you need insulation with an attached vapor barrier? Follow the guidelines on page 87.

> **Exception:** For the area between the collar beams, if you're laying the new insulation on top of old insulation, buy insulation without a vapor barrier if possible, or slash the vapor barrier on the new insulation.

How Thick?

1. For the area between the collar beams, follow the guidelines on page 77. ("Existing insulation" means either insulation between the collar beams or in the attic floor.)

2. For the rafters and end walls, buy insulation that's thick enough to fill up the rafter and stud spaces. If there's some existing insulation in there, the combined thickness of the new and old insulation together should fill up the spaces.

How much

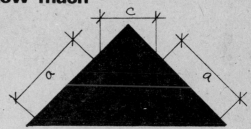

1. Figure out the area you want the insulation to cover between your rafters and collar beams (shown above). In general, figure each area to be covered, and add the areas up. If your attic is like the one shown, measure distances a, b, and c, enter them below, and do the figuring indicated (the .9 allows for the space taken up by rafters or collar beams.):

$$\underline{\hspace{2cm}} \times \underline{\hspace{2cm}} \times .9 = \underline{\hspace{2cm}}$$
distance a   distance b   Area 1

$$\underline{\hspace{2cm}} \times \underline{\hspace{2cm}} \times .9 = \underline{\hspace{2cm}}$$
distance a   distance b   Area 2

$$\underline{\hspace{2cm}} \times \underline{\hspace{2cm}} \times 9 = \underline{\hspace{2cm}}$$
distance b   distance c   Area 3

+

total area of insulation
needed for rafters
collar beams.

2. Calculate the length of 2x4 stock you'll need for collar beams. Measure the length of span you need between rafters (c) and count the number of collar beams you need to install. Multiply to get the length of stock you need. You can have the lumber yard cut it to length at a small charge. If you cut it yourself, allow for waste. If you plan to finish your attic, check with your lumber yard to make sure 2" X 4"'s are strong enough to support the ceiling you plan to install.

3. Figure out the area of each end wall you want to insulate. Measure (d) and (e) and multiply to determine the area. Multiply by (.9) to correct for the space taken up by the studs, then multiply by the number of end walls.

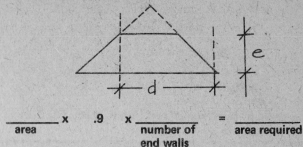

$$\underline{\hspace{1cm}} \; x \; .9 \; x \; \underline{\text{number of}} = \underline{\text{area required}}$$
area   number of
                     end walls

Installation

Preparation

Check for roof leaks, looking for water stains or marks. If you can find any leaks, make repairs before you insulate. Wet insulation is useless and can damage the structure of your house. Determine your need for more ventilation by referring to page 87. Put up your temporary lights and:

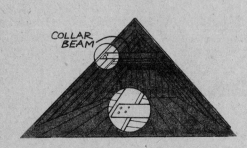

1. Install 2x4 collar beams spanning from rafter to rafter at the ceiling height you want. Every pair of rafters should have a collar beam spanning between them.

   Note: If you're installing new insulation over existing insulation:

   Between the Rafters and Between the End Wall Studs, cut the old insulation loose where it has been stapled, push it to the back of the cavities, and slash the old vapor barrier (if any) before you lay the new insulation over it.

   Between the Collar Beams, lay the new insulation above the old. Lay it over the tops of the collar beams in an unbroken layer at right angles to the beams. Use insulation that does not have a vapor barrier for this part of the job. If you can't get insulation without a vapor barrier, slash the vapor barrier before laying it down, so that moisture won't get trapped in the insulation.

2. Install batts or blanket sections in place between the rafters and collar beams. Install with the vapor barrier on the inside, the side toward you. Don't try to use a continuous length of insulation where the collar beams meet the rafters. It will only result in gaps that are very hard to fill. Install batts in the end walls the same way. Be sure to trim carefully to fit the angles on the end walls.

3. Install batts or blanket sections by stapling the facing flange to the *edge* of the rafter or collar beam. Don't staple to the outside of the rafters; the vapor barrier will have a break at every rafter; and you may compress the insulation against the sheathing, reducing its insulating value.

INSULATE YOUR FINISHED ATTIC

TWO OPTIONS AVAILABLE

(and worth considering if there's under 4 inches of insulation already there.)

1. **Contractor Installation:** insulation blown into the ceiling, sloping rafters and outer attic floors; batts installed in the knee walls.

2. **Do-it-yourself:** installation of batts, blankets or loose fill in all attic spaces you can get to.

Where the insulation needs to be installed

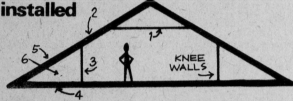

1. Attic Ceiling
2. Rafters
3. Knee Walls
4. Outer Attic Floors, or
5. Outer Attic Rafters
6. End Walls

CONTRACTOR INSTALLED
Types of materials contractors use

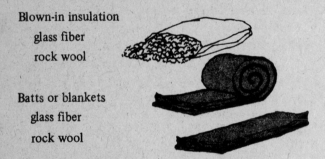

Blown-in insulation
    glass fiber
    rock wool

Batts or blankets
    glass fiber
    rock wool

Preparation

How thick should the insulation be? See page 77.

Check your need for ventilation and a vapor barrier. See page 87.

Check for roof leaks, looking for water stains or marks. If you can find any leaks, make repairs before you insulate. Wet insulation is useless and can damage the structure of your house.

What your contractor will do

Your contractor will blow insulation into the open joist spaces above your attic ceiling, between the rafters, and into the floor of the outer attic space, then install batts in the knee walls. If you want to keep the outer attic spaces heated for storage or any other purpose, you should have the contractor install batts between the outer attic rafters instead of insulating the outer floors and knee walls.

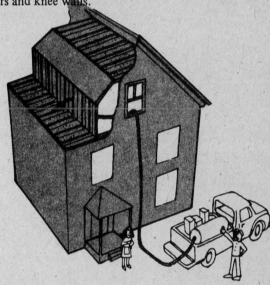

Page 83 describes how blown-in insulation is installed under an unfinished attic floor. This process is much the same for open joists with no floor over them. Pages 84-85 describe the right way to install batts.

DO-IT-YOURSELF

You can insulate wherever you can get into the unfinished spaces.

Installing insulation in your attic ceiling is the same as installing it in an unfinished attic. Look at pages 80-82 to see how this is done.

If you want to insulate your outer attic spaces yourself, install batts between the rafters and the studs in the small triangular end walls. Look at page 85 to see how to do this.

DO YOU NEED A VAPOR BARRIER OR MORE VENTILATION IN YOUR ATTIC?

CONTRACTOR INSTALLED OR DO-IT-YOURSELF

Whenever you add insulation to your house, you should consider the need for a vapor barrier or more ventilation where you're doing the work.

A vapor barrier will prevent water vapor from condensing and collecting in your new insulation or on the beams and rafters of your house.

Added ventilation will remove water vapor before it gets a chance to condense and will also increase summer comfort by cooling off your attic.

What you need

If you're insulating your attic and:

. . . you live in Zone I

1. Install a vapor barrier (unless you are blowing insulation into a finished attic)

2. Add ventilation area equal to 1/300 your attic floor area if:

   Signs of condensation occur after one heating season

   OR

   You can't install a vapor barrier with your insulation

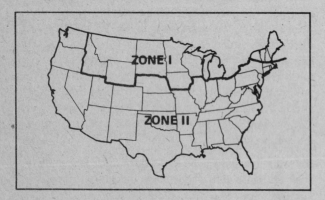

. . . if you live in Zone II and don't have air conditioning

1. Install a vapor barrier toward the living space if you are insulating a finished attic (with other attics a vapor barrier is optional).

2. Add ventilation area equal to 1/300 your attic floor area if signs of condensation occur after one heating season.

. . . you live in Zone II and have air conditioning

1. Install a vapor barrier toward the living space if you are insulating a finished attic (with other attics a vapor barrier is optional).

2. Add ventilation area equal to 1/150 your attic floor area.

What should be installed

Vapor barriers: If you are installing batt or blanket insulation, and you need a vapor barrier, buy the batts or blankets with the vapor barrier attached. Install them with the vapor barrier side toward the living space.

If you are installing a loose fill insulation, lay down polyethylene (heavy, clear plastic) in strips between the joists first.

DON'T BLOCK VENTILATION PATH

Ventilation: Install ventilation louvers (round or rectangular) in the eaves and gables (ridge vents are also available but are more difficult and costly to install in your house). The total open area of these louvers should be either 1/300 or 1/150 of your attic area (see "What You Need" above), and evenly divided between the gables and the eaves.

Ventilation louvers should be installed by a carpenter unless you are an experienced handyman.

Don't Block Ventilation Path with Insulation.

INSULATE YOUR WOOD FRAME WALLS

CONTRACTOR INSTALLED

Normally, insulating material is blown into the spaces in a wood frame wall through holes drilled from the outside or the inside. An alternate procedure uses plastic foam (ureaformaldahyde) to fill the stud spaces.

NOTE: Condensation in insulated walls may be a problem; see box on condensation, p. 60

Types of materials contractors use

Blow-in insulation:
- glass fiber
- rock wool
- cellulosic fiber

Foam-in insulation:

plastic foam installed as a foam under slight pressure which hardens to form insulation. Quality of application to date has been very inconsistent — ask your local HUD/FHA office to recommend a qualified installer.

What your contractor will do

The contractor will measure the area you want insulated to determine how much material he will need and to estimate the cost. To install the insulation, the contractor must be able to get all the spaces in the wall. For each space he must drill a hole, usually in the outside wall, after removing the finished layer (usually clapboard or shingle). This always amounts to a lot of holes, but once the job is complete, a good contractor will leave no traces behind.

If you have brick veneer on the exterior, the procedure is much the same, except that it may be cheaper to do it from the inside.

Once the holes in the wall have been made your contractor is then ready to install the insulation. If the insulation is blow-in insulation he'll be following the process outlined in this book. If he's using foam, he'll pump the foam into the wall spaces through a flexible hose with an applicator. With either method, each space will be completely filled, and the siding replaced.

What you should check

First be very careful about selecting a contractor.

Before you sign an agreement with your contractor, define what you're buying and make sure it's spelled out in the contract. Insulation material properly installed will add an R-Value of 8 for rock wool, 10 for cellulosic fiber, or 11.5 for ureaformaldehyde in a standard wood frame wall. You should agree on what that R-Value is with the contractor before the job begins. Next, check a bag of the type of insulation he intends to use (there will only be bags of mineral fiber or cellulosic fiber — there's no good way to check quantity with foam). On it, there will be a table which will indicate how many square feet of wall space that bag is meant to fill while giving your house the desired R value. The information may be in different forms (number of square feet per bag or number of bags per 1000 square feet), so you may have to do some simple division to use the number correctly.

Knowing this and the area of your walls, you should be able to figure out about how many bags should be installed to give you the desired R-value.

This number should be agreed upon between you and the contractor before the job is begun. While the job is in progress be sure the correct amount is being installed. There's nothing wrong with having the contractor save the empty bags so you can count them — 4 or 5 bags more or less than the amount you agreed on is an acceptable difference from the estimate.

INSULATE YOUR FLOOR

TWO OPTIONS AVAILABLE

1. DO-IT-YOURSELF

Install batts or blankets between the floor joists by stapling wire mesh or chicken wire to the bottom of the joists and sliding the batts or blankets in on top of the wire. Place vapor barrier up.

The job is quite easy to do in most cases. If you are insulating over a crawl space there may be some problems with access or working room, but careful planning can make things go much more smoothly and easily.

Check your floor joist spacing — this method will work best with standard 16" or 24" joist spacing. If you have non-standard or irregular spacing there will be more cutting and fitting and some waste of material.

2. CONTRACTOR INSTALLED

DO-IT-YOURSELF
Tools

1. Heavy duty shears or linoleum knife

2. Temporary lighting with waterproof wiring and connectors

3. Portable fan or blower to provide ventilation

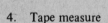
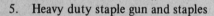

4. Tape measure
5. Heavy duty staple gun and staples

Safety

1. Provide adequate temporary lighting
2. Wear gloves and breathing mask when working with glass fiber or rock wool
3. Provide adequate ventilation
4. Keep lights and all wires off wet ground

Materials
What you'll need

1. R11 (3"-3½") batts or blankets or rock wool or glass fiber, preferably with foil facing (See Installation).

2. Wire mesh or chicken wire of convenient width for handling in tight space.

How much

Determine the area to be insulated by measuring the length and width and multiplying to get the area.

(length) X (width) = area

(_____) X (_____) = _____

You may find it necessary to divide the floor into smaller areas and add them.

(length) X (width) = area

(_____) X (_____) = _____

(_____) X (_____) = _____

(_____) X (_____) = _____ +

total area = _____

(.9)(total area) = area of insulation

(.9)(_____) =   _____

total area = area of wire mesh or chicken wire

Installation

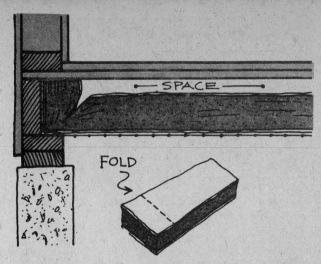

Start at a wall at one end of the joists and work out. Staple the wire to the bottom of the joists, and at right angles to them. Slide batts in on top of the wire. Work with short sections of wire and batts so that it won't be too difficult to get the insulation in place. Plan sections to begin and end at obstructions such as cross bracing.

Buy insulation with a vapor barrier, and install the vapor barrier facing up (next to the warm side) leaving an air space between the vapor barrier and the floor. Get foil-faced insulation if you can; it will make the air space insulate better. Be sure that ends of batts fit snugly up against the bottom of the floor to prevent loss of heat up end. Don't block combustion air openings for furnaces.

CHOOSING A CONTRACTOR

If you decide that a particular home improvement you want to make should be done by a contractor, there are some things you should know about finding the right person for the job. The large majority of contractors take pride in their business, are conscientious, and honest. But you should still spend some time and effort in making your choice, and once the choice is made, in clearly defining the job.

1. Where to start looking

Yellow Pages under "Insulation Contractors — Cold and Heat." Don't be suspicious of the small operation — even just a carpenter and his helper. You're doing a relatively small project and often the small business man will give you an excellent job.

Local Chapter of the National Association of Home Builders or Home Builders Association. They will be very helpful in recommending contractors.

Your banker. It's in his interest to recommend a man who will do a good job if he's loaning you the money to do the work.

Local government offices for government funded or non-profit operated home improvement assistance centers. They don't exist everywhere but the ones that do are interested in helping, and maintain files on contractors that they recommend.

From these sources, establish a list of three or four contractors from which to select.

2. How to select from your list

Ask each contractor for a list of past customers, and check their satisfaction with his work.

See how long each contractor has been in business — in general, the longer the better.

Call your local Better Business Bureau and ask if there have been any complaints against each of the contractors on your list.

Get estimates from each on any job you think will cost more than $200.00.

3. Once you've selected a contractor — put it IN WRITING

Have him write up a specific contract for your job.

Check the contract carefully for work content and warranty. The best way to do this is to make a list of all the things you feel he should do in the course of the job (use the applicable Part III pages for assistance here). Then check what you know should be included against what's in the contract.

Sign the contract only when you are fully satisfied that it details everything you want done. Insisting on a detailed contract doesn't mean that you don't trust your contractor. But once you have a contract, each of you knows his limit of responsibility before the job begins.

INSULATE YOUR BASEMENT WALLS

EXTERIOR WALLS ONLY

A MODERATELY EASY DO-IT-YOURSELF PROJECT

Install 2" X 3" studs along the walls to be insulated. Add glass fiber blanket insulation between the furring strips and finish with wallboard or panelling.

> **NOTE:** The method of insulation shown here should not be used by residents of Alaska, Minnesota, and northern Maine. The extreme frost penetration in these areas can cause heaving of the foundation if the insulation method shown here is used. Residents of these areas should contact local HUD/FHA field offices for advice.

Tools

1. Saw
2. Hammer, nails
3. Heavy duty staple gun, or hammer and tacks
4. Tape measure
5. Linoleum knife or heavy duty shears
6. Level
7. Small sledge hammer, masonry nails

Safety

1. Provide adequate temporary lighting

2. If you use glass fiber or rock wool, wear gloves and a breathing mask, and keep the material wrapped until you are ready to use it

Materials

What you'll need

1. R7 (2-2½ inch) Batt or blanket insulation, glass fiber or rockwool, with a vapor barrier (buy polyethylene if you can't get batts or blankets with a vapor barrier)

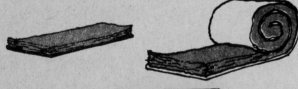

2. 2" X 3" studs

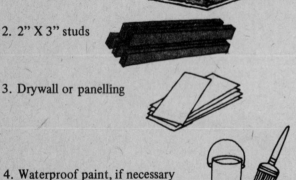

3. Drywall or panelling

4. Waterproof paint, if necessary

How much

1. Find the average height above the ground of the walls you intend to insulate and add two feet. Then measure the length of the walls you intend to insulate. Multiply the two figures to determine how many square feet of insulation is needed.

    (height) X (length) = area

    _____ X _____ = _____

2. Find the linear feet of studs you'll need by multiplying the length of the walls you intend to insulate by (6).

    (6) X (length) = (linear ft.)

    (6) X _____ = _____

3. The area of wall covering equals the basement wall height times the length of wall you intend to finish.

    (height) X (length) = area

    _____ X _____ = _____

Installation

Preparation

Check to see whether or not moisture is coming through your basement walls from the ground outside. If it is and your walls are damp, you should eliminate the cause of the dampness to prevent the insulation you're going to install from becoming wet and ineffective.

Nail the bottom plate to the floor at the base of the wall with a hammer and concrete nails. Install studs 16 or 24 inches apart after the top plate is nailed to the joists above. (Where the wall runs parallel to the joists, nail the top plate to the tops of the studs, and fasten the studs to the wall.)

Cut blankets into sections long enough to extend from the top plate to 2 feet below the ground line. Staple them into place between the studs, with the vapor barrier towards the living space. **NOTE:** in northern climates there will be added benefit to installing the insulation the full height of the wall.

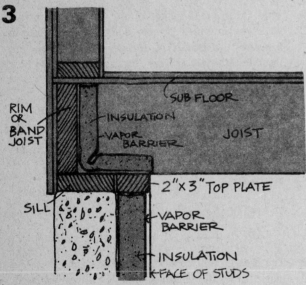

Install another small piece of insulation above the furring and against the sill to insulate the sill and band joist.

Install finish wall board or panelling over insulation and furring.

MEASUREMENTS
WORKSHEET SUMMARY

1. WINDOWS AND DOORS

Number of windows
requiring storms   no._____ avg._____ sf

Fit of windows   average_____ loose_____

Existing glazing   single_____double_____double_____
                                    sealed   unsealed

Picture window   yes_____ no_____ size_____ sf

Number of doors
requiring storms   no. _____.

Fit of door   avg._____ loose_____

Existing door type   wood_____wood_____metal_____
                          solid   hollow   insulated

Comments   _____

                          _____

2. CEILING/ATTIC

Existing insulation   _____inches

Gross area   _____sf

Attic access   _____

Attic condition   pitch_____

                          flooring _____ %

                          storage_____
                          ventilation
                          existing_____

Comments   _____

                          _____

                          _____

3. EXTERIOR WALLS

Existing insulation   _____

Siding type   _____

Sheathing   _____

Gross wall area   _____sf

Glass and door area   proportion: normal_____ higher_____

Comments   _____

                          _____

4. BASEMENT/CRAWL SPACE

Gross exterior wall
area   _____sf

Percentage exposed
to outside   ¼_____ ½_____ ¾_____

Gross basement area   _____sf

Gross crawl space   area _____ sf

Number of windows
requiring storms   no._____

Comments   _____

                          _____

                          _____

5. HEATING/COOLING SYSTEM

Furnace   Description_____

                          Filter size_____
                          Tune-up
                          req's._____

A/C   Description_____
                          Tune up
                          req's._____

Ducts   lineal
                          feet and size_____

                          insulated: yes_____ no_____

Humidifier   yes_____ no_____

Thermostat setting   winter: day_____ night_____

                          summer: day_____ night_____

6. MISCELLANEOUS

_____

_____

_____

_____

_____

_____

_____

_____

COSTS WORKSHEET SUMMARY

ITEMS	SPECIFICATIONS	COST
WINDOWS AND DOORS		
1. STORM WINDOWS	Install_____ storm windows, model_____ cost_____ each	$_____
2. PICTURE WINDOW	Install storm sash _____	$_____
3. STORM DOORS	Install_____ storm doors, model_____ cost_____ each	$_____
4. EXTERIOR DOORS	Weatherstrip_____ exterior doors_____	$_____
CEILING ATTIC		
5. CEILING INSULATION	Add_____ inches_____ insulation for certified R-_____ value cost ($_____/sf) × (_____sf) = _____	$_____
6. ATTIC VENTILATION	Describe _____	$_____
7. ATTIC ACCESS	Add insulated opening_____ sf _____	$_____
EXTERIOR WALLS		
8. INSULATION	Add_____ insulation for certified R-_____ value_____ cost ($_____/sf) × (_____sf) = _____	$_____
OTHER	Describe _____	$_____
BASEMENT/CRAWL SPACE		
9. FLOOR INSULATION	Install insulation over unconditioned spaces _____	$_____
10. EXTERIOR WALLS	Seal all openings and cracks _____	$_____
11. BASEMENT WINDOWS	Install_____ storm windows, model_____ cost_____ each	$_____
OTHER	R-batts between joists ($_____/sf) × (_____sf) = _____	$_____
FURNACE/AC		
12. UNCONDITIONED AREAS	Tape joints and insulate ducts _____	$_____
13. FURNACE/AC	Tune up cost_____, 1-year supply filters cost_____	$_____
14. CLOCK THERMOSTAT	Install thermostat model _____	$_____
15. HUMIDIFIER	Install model _____	$_____
16. WATER HEATER	Replace with new model _____	$_____
17. AC UNIT	Replace with new unit _____	$_____
18. CEILING FAN	Install _____	$_____
19. FURNACE	Replace with proper unit _____	$_____
20. MISCELLANEOUS	_____	$_____
21. CUSTOM	_____	$_____
TOTAL COST		$_____

SAVING ENERGY WITH YOUR HEATING, AIR CONDITIONING & WATER HEATING

TWO OPTIONS AVAILABLE

1. **Routine Servicing** — your serviceman should check all your heating and cooling equipment and do any needed maintenance once a year.

2. **Repair or Replacement** — some of your heating and cooling equipment may be so badly worn or outmoded that it will pay you to replace it now and get your money back in a few years.

Routine Servicing

A periodic checkup and maintenance of your heating and cooling equipment can reduce your fuel consumption by about 10 per cent. Locating a good heating/cooling specialist and sticking with him is a good way to ensure that your equipment stays in top fuel-saving condition. Your local fuel supplier or heating/cooling system repair specialist are the people to call — you can find them in the Yellow Pages under:

Heating Contractors
Air Conditioning Equipment
Furnaces-Heating

Electric Heating
Oil Burner-Equipment
and Service

Check out the people you contact with the Better Business Bureau and other homeowners in your area. Once you're satisfied you're in touch with a reputable outfit, a *service contract* is the best arrangement to make. For an annual fee, this gets you a periodic tuneup of your heating/cooling system, and insures you against repairs of most components. A regular arrangement like this is the best one — the serviceman gets to know your system, and you're assured of regular maintenance from a company you know.

In this section, there are lists of items your serviceman should check for each type of heating or cooling system. Some items may vary from brand to brand, but *go over the list with your serviceman*. Also listed here are service items you can probably take care of yourself and save even more money. If you don't want to service your system yourself, *make sure* you add those items to your serviceman's list.

Repair or Replacement

. . . of your equipment may be necessary.

When you are faced with major repairs, inevitably the question comes up: should we fix what we've got, or buy new equipment? It's an important question but not difficult to answer if you consider the right things:

1. Get several estimates — the larger the job the more estimates. The special knowledge of the equipment dealer and installer is most needed here — they'll study your house, measure the walls and windows, and should give you *written* estimates.

2. Check to see what your fuel costs are now.

3. Ask each contractor who gives you an estimate to tell you how many years he thinks it will take before the amount you save by having the new system equals what you paid for it. Remember, fuel costs are going up.

Furnace Maintenance

OIL BURNER

Every Year

Adjust and clean burner unit

Adjust fuel-to-air ratio for maximum efficiency

Check for oil leaks

Check electrical connections, especially on safety devices

Clean heating elements and surfaces

Adjust dampers and draft regulator

Change oil filters

Change air filter

Change oil burner nozzle

Check oil pump

Clean house thermostat contacts and adjust

There are several tests servicemen can use to check oil furnace efficiency:

Draft Test to see if heat is being lost up the chimney or if draft is not enough to properly burn your oil.

Smoke Test to see if your oil is being burned cleanly and completely.

CO_2 test to see if fuel is being burned completely.

Stack Temperature Test to see if stack gases are too hot or not hot enough.

COAL FURNACE

At the end of each heating season

Adjust and clean stoker

Clean burner of all coal, ash and clinkers

Oil the inside of the coal screw and hopper to prevent rust

GAS FURNACE (bottled, LP or natural)

Every 3 Years

Check operation of main gas valve, pressure regulator, and safety control valve

Adjust primary air supply nozzle for proper combustion

Clean thermostat contacts and adjust for proper operation

See Draft Test and Stack Temperature Test above

ELECTRIC FURNACE

Very little maintenance required. Check the manufacturers specifications.

Heat Distribution Systems

Some items here you can do yourself to keep your system at top efficiency. For the ones you can't, check above on how to pick a serviceman. Note: except where it says otherwise, these are all once a year items.

HOT WATER HEATING SYSTEM

Serviceman:

Check pump operation

Check operation of flow control valve

Check for piping leaks

Check operation of radiator valves

Drain and Flush the boiler

Oil Pump Motor

You can do this yourself:

Bleed air from the system. Over time, a certain amount of air will creep into the pipes in your system. It will find its way to the radiators at the top of your house, and wherever there's air, it keeps out hot water. There's usually a small valve at the top of each radiator. *Once or twice a year* open the valve at each radiator. Hold a bucket under it, and keep the valve open until the water comes out. Watch out, the water is *hot*.

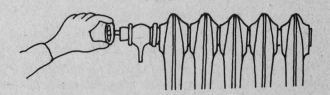

Draining and Flushing the boiler is also something you can do yourself. Ask your serviceman to show you how.

FORCED HOT AIR HEATING SYSTEM

Once a Year

Serviceman:

Check blower operation

Oil the blower motor if it doesn't have sealed bearings.

Check for duct leaks where duct is accessible.

You can do these yourself:

Clean or replace air filters — *this is important,* easy to do, and is something that needs to be done more often than it pays to have a serviceman do it. Every 30 to 60 days during the heating season you should clean or replace (depending on whether they're disposable) the air filters near the furnace in your system. Ask your serviceman how to do it, buy a supply, and stick to a schedule — you can save a lot of fuel this way.

Clean the fan blade that moves the air through your system — it gets dirty easily and won't move the air well unless it's clean. Do this every year.

Keep all registers clean — Vacuum them every few weeks. Warm air coming out of the registers should have a free path unobstructed by curtains or furniture.

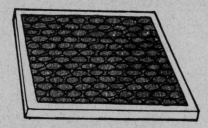

STEAM HEAT SYSTEM

With steam heat, if your serviceman checks your burner, (see Furnace Maintenance above) and the water system in your boiler, most of his work is done. There are two things you can do to save energy, though:

Insulate steam pipes that are running through spaces you don't want to heat.

Every 3 weeks during the heating season, drain a bucket of water out of your boiler (your serviceman will show you how) — this keeps sediment off the bottom of the boiler. If the sediment is allowed to stay there, it will actually *insulate* your boiler from the flame in your burner and a lot of heat will go up the chimney that would have heated your home.

Whole–House Air Conditioning

Once a Year

(Got room air conditioners?— many of these hints apply, ask your dealer about what you can do to your room air conditioners)

Serviceman:

Oil bearings on fan and compressor if they are not sealed

Measure electrical current drawn by compressor

Check pulley belt tension

Check for refrigerating fluid leaks and add fluid if needed

Check electrical connections

Re-adjust dampers — if your air conditioner uses the same ducts as your heating system, different settings are usually required for summer cooling than for winter heating.

Flush evaporator drain line.

You Can Do These Yourself

Clean or replace air filters — *this is important,* and if done every 30 to 60 days will save you far more money in fuel than the cost of the filters.

Clean the condenser coils of dust, grass clippings, etc.

NOTE: Your condenser is the part of your air conditioner that sits outside your house. It should be shaded — if it has to work in the sun it wastes a lot of fuel. When you shade it, make sure you don't obstruct the flow of air out and around it.

Duct Insulation

If the ducts for either your heating or your air conditioning system run exposed through your attic or garage (or any other space that is not heated or cooled) they should be insulated. Duct insulation comes generally in blankets 1 or 2" thick. Get the thicker variety, particularly if you've got rectangular ducts. If you're doing this job at all, it's worth it to do it right. For air conditioning ducts, make sure you get the kind of insulation that has a vapor barrier (the vapor barrier goes on the outside). Seal the joints of the insulation tightly with tape to avoid condensation.

NOTE: Check for leaks in the duct and tape them — tightly before insulating.

Heating water with your air conditioner

The part of the whole-house air conditioner that sits outside your house gives off a tremendous amount of heat. If your house is centrally air conditioned and you live far enough south so that your system runs more than 3 months out of the year, there's a way to use the energy the air conditioner gives off to heat your domestic hot water. A simple device is fitted to your air conditioner, and pipes run from your water heater. The installed cost of this is significant, but you get it back over time in free hot water that is heated by your air conditioner. Call your electric company or an air conditioning repairman to see if this energy saver is available in your area.

Air conditioning

Closing off unused rooms is just as important in saving on air conditioning as it is for heating. Keep lights off during the day—most of the electricity they use makes heat, not light. You also can reduce the load on your air conditioning system by not using heat-generating appliances like your dishwasher during the hot part of the day (or stop the dishwasher when the drying cycle begins).

If you have central air conditioning, you may want to look into the *air economizer*, a system which turns off the part of your air conditioner that uses a lot of electricity, and circulates outside air through the house when it's cooler out than it is in. By using the cooler outside air, the system reduces its own job and saves money for you. Ask your air-conditioning dealer if he can install one on your system.

Buying a room air conditioner

When you go to buy a room air-conditioning unit, check the EER—Energy Efficiency Ratio. The higher the EER number, the less electricity the unit will use to cool the same amount of air—you should consider your possible fuel savings when deciding how much to spend on your air

conditioning unit. A unit which costs more to begin with may save enough money over the next summer to make it worth it.

Typical EER's available range from 4 to 12; a unit with an EER of 4 will cost about 3 times as much to operate as one with an EER of 12.

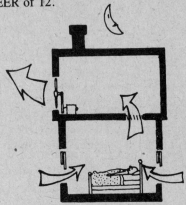

One alternative to energy-consuming air conditioning is the use of an *attic fan* to cool your home. Normally a house holds heat, so that there's a lag between the time the outside air cools after sunset on a summer night and the time that the house cools. The purpose of the attic fan is to speed up the cooling of the house by pulling air in through open windows up through the attic and out.

When the fan's on, you can let air through to the attic either by opening the attic door part way or by installing a louver that does the same thing automatically.

In a part of the country that has hot days and cool nights, using an attic fan in the evenings and closing the windows and curtains during the day can *replace* air conditioning. The *size* of the fan you buy should be determined by the amount of space you want to cool. You can figure out the fan size you need by finding the *volume* of your house: Rounding off to the nearest foot, multiply the length of your house by its width, then multiply by its height (from the ground to just below the attic). This will give you the volume in *cubic feet*. The capacity of all fans is marked on the fan in *CFM's*—*C*ubic *F*eet of air moved per *M*inute. Divide the volume of your house by 10; this will give you the CFM rating of the fan you need to change the air in the house 6 times an hour.

volume of house	÷ 10 =	CFM fan rating

Heat Build-up in the Attic Space

In the summer the sun's heat adds a large radiant heat load to the air-conditioning system. This heat will build up and be stored even through a cool summer night. Radiant heat plus stored-up heat means high summer air-conditioning bills plus strain on all components of the air-conditioning system. Adequate ventilation of attic spaces can dramatically reduce both factors and lead to both longer life for the air-conditioning system and reduced bills for electricity.

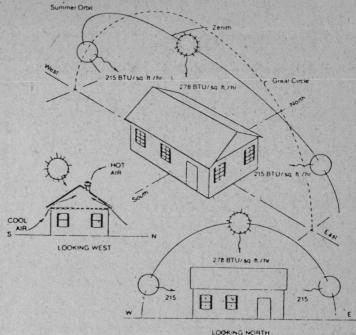

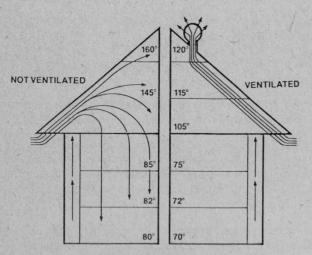

These figures represent the solar radiation intensity hitting a residence located in Kansas City, Mo. (39° N. Lat.), June 21, 1973, at 12 noon. For a 2000 ft²

house with a solar radiation intensity at noon of 278 Btu/ft²/h there is a heat gain of 2000 ft² times 278 Btu/ft²/h equalling 556,000 Btu/h. One ton of air conditioning equals 12,000 Btu/h. If all the radiant heat from the sun were to be absorbed by the house, it would take 556,000 Btu/h divided by 12,000 Btu/h equalling 46 tons of refrigeration to keep the house at 70° F. Why does it not take 46 tons? Part of the heat is reflected. Part is removed by convection. Part of the heat is stopped by insulation at the ceiling line. The reason attic ventilators do such a dramatic job is because there is so much heat left between the roof and the ceiling available to be dissipated by air removal.

For maximum flow induction, a ventilator should be located on that part of the roof where it will receive the full wind without interference. If roof ventilators are installed within the suction region created by the wind passing over the roof, their performance will be greatly increased.

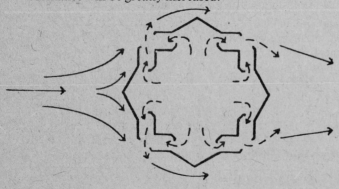

Wind creating aspirating action in roof ventilator.

Types of roof ventilators

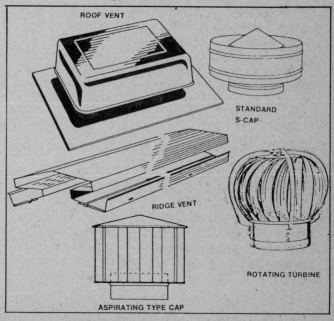

PART 6: MORE ON HOW TO SAVE ENERGY

The ethics of energy conservation

Yesterday's Home

In yesterday's home energy was visible. The earliest homes were heated with wood and lit by candles and oil lamps.

By looking at the size of the wood pile the homeowner could see the amount of energy available. The log burning showed energy being used. The source of energy used for heating, cooking, and lighting was visible.

In yesterday's home the homeowner was the worker as well as the natural conserver. He brought in as much wood as he needed, and he seldom wasted it since he would have to chop more if he did. The lamp had to be refilled when it was empty so he was careful to turn it off when it was not needed. He was part of the energy cycle. More important, the cycle was one that he could visualize.

Today's Home

Let's look at the mechanical revolutions that have occurred in housing in the last 70 years. First came central heating fired by coal furnaces with hot water and steam radiators.

Then came natural gas piped into the house to fire stoves and hot water heaters as well as central heating systems.

Finally, the development of electricity as an energy source led us to today's use of an ever-increasing range of appliances from air-conditioners to electric toothbrushes.

Even with the coal furnace, energy was still visible and the homeowner was still a participant.

He shoveled the coal from the bin, saw it burn, and banked the fire at night. When the furnace was converted to oil or natural gas, a drastic change took place. The energy source was not visible anymore, nor was the homeowner needed in the energy cycle. More importantly, he was no longer the natural conserver. All he had to do was to pay the bills, and they seemed very modest.

Today with the cost of fuels increasing and the supply of those fuels decreasing, the homeowner must once again become the conserver. By building or retrofitting his home to conserve energy, and by using and maintaining the mechanical systems in it efficiently, he can keep his energy costs down.

By understanding how the utility meters work he will know what the bills are for.

Energy consumption in the United States

This nation uses more energy per capita than any other nation in the world. Although we have only about 6% of the world's population, we use 35% of all the energy consumed in the world.

Since most homes were built in the days when energy was plentiful and cheap, even as simple an "improvement" as setting the thermostat no higher than 68°F in winter and no lower than 78°F in summer will save a surprising amount of energy.

In the heating season alone, adequate insulation in the attic floor generally will save up to 20% on fuel bills.

In your case, the percentage of savings will depend upon how much insulation you had before you added more, the attic area of your house in relation to wall area, number and size of windows and doors, and whether you have storm windows and doors and good weather stripping.

The exact amount of money you will save is affected, of course, by rates you pay for fuel and electricity. However, no matter what those rates are, if you make energy-conserving improvements to your home now, you can expect even greater future dollar savings as energy costs rise with inflation.

Most observers view energy conservation as a helpmate to environmental quality. Usually the two go hand-in-hand. It has been extravagant use of energy that has pushed man toward heavy exploitation of his natural resources. Domestic oil shortages are forcing us to turn more to coal as an energy source. Eventually, research will almost certainly lead to development of cleaner ways to mine and burn coal. Research also will lead to greater utilization of energy sources such as geothermal power, solar energy, and others not yet in widespread use and will be both economically and environmentally acceptable. Development of more efficient gasoline engines, improved insulation of buildings, and new industrial processes will enable us to maintain our standard of living with lower energy expenditure. Less energy growth means important environmental savings. Truly, a barrel saved is worth *more* than a barrel found.

"Nature never gives anything away. Everything is sold at a price. It is only in the ideals of abstraction that choice comes without consequence."
—*Ralph Waldo Emerson*

100

Year-round energy saver

Rising energy costs make these ever-more sensible.
Cooking and heating the Nation's households in 1974 is expected to consume about 11% of all the energy that will be used in the United States throughout the year. Lighting consumes over 16% of all electricity used in American homes.

It is these energy-intensive household operations where waste often is found, and where you can save considerable amounts of energy and reduce family expenses accordingly. Consider the following all-weather conservation measures:

Close off unoccupied rooms and turn off the heat or air-conditioning.
Use bath and kitchen ventilating fans only as needed.
Repair all leaky faucets, especially hot water faucets, as quickly as possible.
Insulate hot water storage tank and piping.
Turn off radio and television sets when not in use.
"Instant-on" television sets, especially the tube types, use energy even when the screen is dark. To eliminate this waste, plus the set into an outlet that is controlled by a wall switch; turn the set on and off with the switch. Or ask your TV serviceman to install an additional on-off switch on the set itself or in the cord to the outlet.
Do as much household cleaning as possible with cold water. This saves energy used to heat water (and some cleaning products work better in cold water).
If you have a fireplace, be sure the damper is closed except when the fire is going, otherwise heated or cooled air goes wastefully up the chimney.

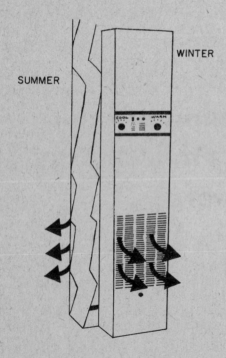

Shading your home

A good way to keep your house cool in the summer is to shade it from the outside. The east and west sides are where the most heat comes through—if you can shade it here it'll show up right away in a smaller air conditioning bill and a cooler home. Any way that stops the sun before it gets in through the glass is *seven times* as good at

keeping you cool as blinds and curtains on the inside. So trees and vines that shade in the summer and lose their leaves for the winter are what you want—they'll let the sun back in for the winter months. If you can't shade your house with trees concentrate on keeping the sun out of your windows—awnings or even permanent sunshades will do the job (but only on the south side; they won't work on the east and west).

Hot weather energy savers

Some special summer, or warm climate saving tips:
Set air-conditioning thermostats no lower than 78°.
The 78° temperature is judged to be reasonably comfortable and energy efficient. One authority estimates that if this setting raises the temperature 6° (78° vs 72°) home cooling costs should drop about 47%. (The Federal Government is enforcing a strict 78-80° temperature in all its buildings during the summer.)

If everyone raised cooling thermostats 6° during the summer, the Nation would save more than the equivalent of 36 billion kilowatt hours of electricity, or 2% of the Nation's total electricity consumption for a year.

Run air conditioners only on really hot days and set the fan speed at high. In very humid weather, set the fan at low speed to provide less cooling but more moisture removal. Clean or replace air conditioner filters at least once a month. Turning the fan requires more electricity when the filter is dirty.

If you can confine your living spaces to fewer rooms, close off the rooms that will not be occupied.
If rooms are to be unoccupied for several hours, turn off the air-conditioning temporarily.

Buy the cooling equipment with the smallest capacity to do the job. More cooling power than necessary is inefficient and expensive. Energy-efficiency ratios (EERs) for most air-conditioning units should be available from dealers, and some window units are labeled to show the EER (the higher the EER, the more efficient the air conditioner). If you don't see a label in the showroom, ask for the information.

Additional hot weather energy savers

Deflect daytime sun with vertical louvers or awnings on windows, or draw draperies and shades in sunny windows. Keep windows and outside doors closed during the hottest hours of the day.

Keep the lights low or off. Electric lights generate heat and add to the load on the air conditioning equipment.

Use vents and exhaust fans to pull heat and moisture from attics, kitchens, and laundries directly to the outside.

Do as much cooking as possible, and use heat-generating equipment, in the early morning and late evening hours. On cooler days and during cooler hours, open the windows instead of using air-conditioner or electric fans.

Turn off the furnace pilot light. But be sure it is re-ignited before you turn the furnace on again.

Dress for the higher temperatures. Neat but casual clothes of lightweight fabrics are most comfortable for men and women and are acceptable almost everywhere during the summer.

Cold weather energy savers

To save on heating energy and heating costs:
Lower thermostats to 68° during the day and 60° at night. If these settings reduce the temperature an average of 6°, heating costs should run about 15% less.

If every household in the United States lowered heating temperatures 6°, the demand for fuel would drop by more than 570,000 barrels of oil per day (enough to heat over 9 million homes during the winter season).

Setting nighttime temperatures back can reduce heating costs significantly. Consider the advantages of a clock thermostat which will automatically turn the heat down at a regular hour before you retire and turn it up just before you wake.
Have your furnace serviced once a year, preferably each fall. Adjustment could mean a saving of 10% in family fuel consumption.

When buying a new furnace, select one that incorporates an automatic flue gas damper, a device which reduces loss of heat when the furnace is not in operation.

If you use electric heating, consider a "heat pump" system. The heat pump uses outside air in both heating and cooling and can cut the use of electricity for heating by 60% or more.

Additional cold weather energy savers

Clean or replace the filter in forced-air heating systems every month.

Dust or vacuum radiator surfaces frequently.
Keep draperies and shades open in sunny windows; close them at night.

For comfort in cooler indoor temperatures use the best insulation of all—warm clothing.

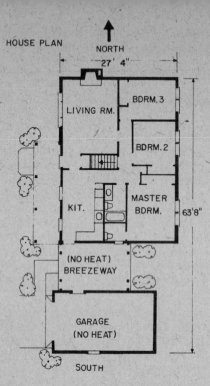

HOUSE PLAN

NORTH

27' 4"

LIVING RM.

BDRM. 3

BDRM. 2

KIT.

MASTER BDRM.

63'8"

(NO HEAT) BREEZEWAY

GARAGE (NO HEAT)

SOUTH

The heat pump

A heat pump runs on electricity, and is just like an air conditioner, except it can run in reverse—it can use electricity to heat, and gets more heat out of a dollar's worth of electricity than the resistance heaters in baseboard units and electric furnaces.

How? There's heat in the air outside your home, even when the temperture's below freezing, and a heat pump can get that warmth out and into your house. When should you consider installing one?—If you presently have a central electric heating system, and live south of Pennsylvania, it may pay to install a heat pump in the system, next to the furnace. Keep your electric furnace—once the temperature drops below 20° or so, the heat pump will need help from the furnace. Installation of a heat pump large enough for most houses should cost a little under $3,000, but you're getting central air conditioning as well as a "furnace" that's about 1½ times more efficient than your electric furnace.

If you're adding a room, consider adding a heat pump—like air conditioners they come in room size units. A heat pump for a room comes with its own electric resistance coil (like a baseboard electric heater) for the times of the year when it's too cold for the heat pump itself to work well. Call your air conditioner dealer for details on both central and room-size heat pumps. If your furnace runs on gas or oil, and the prices of those fuels continue to rise faster than the price of electricity, then you'll want to consider a heat pump too.

Home-Planning— Where energy- wasting mistakes can be avoided

When designing a new house, consider the climate and check local authorities on building codes.

A recommended energy-efficient ratio for window areas is no more than 10% of the floor area. In cool climates, install fewer windows in the north wall where no solar heating gain can be achieved in winter. In warm climates, put the largest number of windows in the north and east walls to reduce the heating gain from the sun.

Install windows you can open, so that you can use natural ventilation in moderate weather.

Use double-pane glass throughout the house. Windows with double-pane heat-reflecting or heat-absorbing glass in south and west windows provide additional energy savings.

Insulate walls and roof to the highest specifications recommended for your area, but provide a minimum of 6'' in the attic and 3'' in the walls. Insulate floors, too, especially those over cold basements and garages.

When buying a new water heater, select one with thick insulation on the shell. Avoid purchasing a tank with greater capacity than needed. Have the dealer advise you on the size suitable for the number of people in your family.

Install water heater as close as possible to areas of major use to minimize heat loss through the pipes; insulate pipes.

Install louvered panels or wind-powered roof ventilators rather than motor-driven fans to ventilate the attic.

If the base of a house—especially a mobile home—is exposed, build a "skirt" around it.

Add a Small Porch

Building a small porch around the door on the south side of your house can really be fun. It has many uses, too. The little porch saves heat. It acts as an air block in the winter, keeping the wind from blowing cold air into the house each time you open the door. With windows built into the three other sides of the porch, it's nice and warm when the sun shines—a good place to dry out wet shoes and overcoats. In the winter, it's a good storage space for firewood. Come spring, the warmth from the sun through the windows makes it a great little greenhouse.

First, check the local building codes. Building the porch should be easy and inexpensive. Keep your porch small. It's small enough that you can use scrap materials and it doesn't need to be insulated.

Start by making two foundation footings of stone or brick. They should stick up about 4'' above the ground and go

deep enough to make a strong support. Now build the porch floor about six feet by six feet with some old beams and plywood. The walls can be made with scrap two-by-fours, some old siding and storm windows. These and other materials for the roof can be purchased very cheaply at a garage sale or auction.

The easiest roof to work with is one that is pitched. Make it steep enough so it doesn't collect too much snow. When you build the porch, don't worry about insulation unless you want to use it as a workroom in the winter. It's important, though, that it be tightly constructed so the wind can't blow in. Caulking around all the seams will be a big help. And when you're done, don't forget to close in around the foundation with dirt.

When buying a house

Select light colored roofing in warm climates.

Ask for a description of the insulation and data on the efficiency of space heating, air-conditioning and water heating plants, or have an independent engineer advise you about the efficiency of the equipment provided. It is a good idea to ask to see the heating bills for the previous year, but remember to adjust for current rates and costs. Consider the need for additional insulation or replacement of equipment. If improvements are necessary, you may want to seek an adjustment in the purchase price to cover all, or a reasonable share, of the costs.

The window heater

The heater is made of a wooden box with a glass top. It fits into your window. The box is divided into an upper and a lower section by a plywood sheet which is painted black on top. As the sun comes through the glass, the air over the black plywood is heated and flows into the house. This pulls cooler house air from the floor into the heater, where it also is heated.

The most important part of building this solar air heater is to insulate it well. Otherwise, the sun's heat will go out the top and sides of the heater rather than into the house. Be sure the glass top is sealed in place with caulking all the way around. Also be sure that the bottom and the sides of the heater have enough insulation.

To build the heater, first build an outer shell just wide enough to make a tight fit inside your south window. You can use 1'' x 10'' lumber for the sides and ⅜'' exterior plywood for the bottom. Make sure all seams are tight and will keep out moisture. Now build another smaller shell so there is space enough to fit 3'' of fiberglass or mineral wool insulation between the two shells. The insulation must cover the sides *and bottom* of the box. The second shell can be made from ¼'' interior grade plywood. Put the insulation in the large shell and fit the smaller shell in place with some wood spacers between the two shells.

Now add the black plywood divider to this box. Leave a 4'' space at the foot of the heater so the air can get around to be heated. To make this divider, use a sheet of ¼'' interior plywood. Measure it to fit across the inside shell. Paint the top of the plywood with flat black paint. Now build some supports with furring strips so that the divider will lie about 2'' below the top of the box. Nail the divider into place.

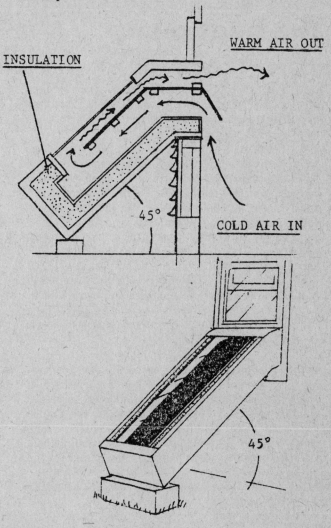

With this divider in the box, you are almost finished. Next, add a piece of 1'' x 10'' wood for the window to rest on when closed. This piece stretches over the whole width of the box and is nailed to the top of the 1'' x 10'' sides of the larger shell. Add a small plywood apron where the bottom section comes into the house. This makes sure that *only* cool air from the floor gets pulled into the heater. To do this, first cover the insulation that shows inside the house. Then stretch a piece of plywood across the mouth of the heater so that it seals tightly against the divider.

The final step is to add the glass cover to the heater. First make wooden cover strips from 1'' pine, wide enough to close in the insulation between the two shells. Measure these pieces to fit in place. Before you nail them in, make a groove along the lengths of the wood in which to lay the glass. Next, nail these on the outer shell so they cover the insulation and the inside shell. Measure for the glass once these are in place. It may be easier and cheaper to use two or three pieces of glass to cover the heater, rather than one larger sheet. If you do, you must nail one or two wood frames across the heater's width, for the glass to rest on. Then have the glass cut to fit. Place it on and hold it in place with glazier points. Don't putty it. Instead, caulk it all the way around the edge so you get a really tight seal.

Just one more step: Paint the wood with house paint before you put the heater in your window. When you use it, be sure to get a tight fit around the window.

Close off the openings at night with some cloth, then pull your window curtain closed. During the summer, take the window heater out and store it in the cellar.

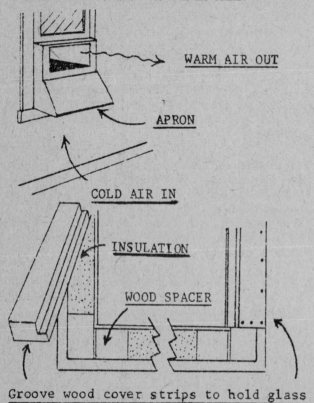

WARM AIR OUT

APRON

COLD AIR IN

INSULATION

WOOD SPACER

Groove wood cover strips to hold glass

Heat from the Sun

You can get the sun's heat by building special solar heaters into your house.

These heaters draw cool house air from the floor into a place where it is heated up by the sun, then push the warmed air back into the house. There are two ways to build them. One kind can be added to your windows, and the other kind makes use of the walls between the windows. Even if your house faces a little to the east or west of true south, they will still work. If you build a solar heater, you will be surprised at how much extra heat you can get—almost enough to heat one whole room of your house on sunny winter days.

The Solar Wall Heater

This type of solar heater makes use of the wall space on the south side of your house. It costs less to build than the other heater, but you must cut some holes in your wall to let cold air in at the bottom and warm air out at the top.

To make one of these heaters, first try to get some old storm windows. This way the glass won't cost much. Once you have the windows, keep them in their frames. Plan the size of the wall heater so that the window frames will just cover the front of the heater.

Now, clean the part of the house wall which the heater will cover. Screw 2'' x 4'''s flat on the wall to make a box around this space. If you have a brick or concrete wall, attach the 2'' x 4'''s with masonry anchors. Paint the wall inside the 2'' x 4'''s with flat black paint.

Next, build a box butting up against the outside of the 2'' x 4'''s. Use 1'' x 6'' lumber. Seal at the edge where it meets the house with caulking, to close any cracks. Put some concrete blocks or bricks beneath the heater to hold up its weight. Then make a box of ¼'' plywood to fit *inside* the 2'' x 4'''s. It should be only 4'' deep. Place 3'' of fiberglass or mineral wool insulation between the two boxes and cover the top with 1'' lumber. Nail this cover in place through the outer side of the large box.

Make vent holes at the top and bottom of the heater for air to come in and out. If your heater is about 3 feet wide, a hole at the top and another at the bottom, about 4'' deep by 14'' wide, will work fine. If it is 6 feet wide, you will need two sets of holes spaced about 3 feet apart.

Now, put the storm windows over the front of the box. If you can get enough of these, make double panes for more efficiency. Use spacers where the storm windows meet and screw them in place. Caulk all around the edges. Paint the outside with house paint—and you're finished!

You will want to close the hole on top at night so warm house air doesn't cool off. Just stuff some cloth into it. When the snows come, shovel snow around the front of

the wall heater. It will reflect sunlight into it. A reflector made with old mirrors or old printing plates stapled to a plywood sheet will help even more.

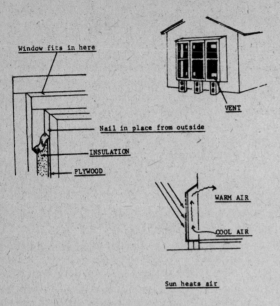

Window fits in here

Nail in place from outside

INSULATION

PLYWOOD

VENT

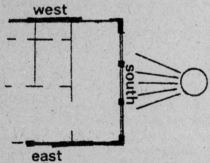

WARM AIR

COOL AIR

Sun heats air

Let the Sun Shine In

Use the sun when there is a clear day in winter. The windows on the south side get the most light. Windows on the east and west sides also get some. From the east, sunlight comes more in the morning. On the west side, you will get afternoon sun. Open curtains and blinds and let this sun come into the house. Make sure that there is nothing near these windows which will block the light from coming into the room.

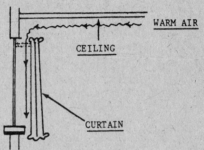

west

south

east

If there are screens on these sunny windows, remove them for the winter so they don't block the sun. Try to work and relax in the sunny rooms during the day. They are the warmest rooms in the house and the extra heat is free.

Use Curtains

To make the best use of sunny windows, you must close them off when the sun is not shining. Curtains should be put up, then closed off at night. This is very important. Windows lose heat to the out-of-doors very quickly. They can rob you of heat two or three times faster than even an uninsulated wall of the same size! So when the sun goes down, button up these windows with curtains.

Another time to curtain off a window is during the summer. Also, put your screens back on in summer. They block some of the light as well as keeping out insects. If you have awnings, use them. They shade the window and keep the house cooler.

Make a Good Window Curtain

Good window curtains will help save you money. They reflect heat back into the house and keep warm air away from the cold window. To do this, the curtain *must* be tight at the top and sides! Otherwise, the warm air at the ceiling will move down the walls and windows as it cools. So button up the curtain on the top and sides and you will have a great heat-saver.

WARM AIR

CEILING

CURTAIN

The curtain should also be light-colored, to reflect back more heat into the house. The curtain material doesn't have to be very heavy—just thick enough so air can't go through it easily. A bedsheet would be too light and let air pass through, but an old wool blanket would be fine.

You can make your own curtain and cheaply too. Make it so that it seals air out of the top and sides when it is closed. Here is the way to do it. To make the top "cap" for the curtain, attach a piece of material to the window frame several inches above the curtain rod area. It should drape over the top of the curtain all the way around. Cut the material so there are no ruffles. The "cap" should lie flat on top of the curtain to make a good air seal. Also, when you tack the cap to the window frame, make sure it seals well.

Tack and seal one side of the curtain to the window frame. On sunny winter days the curtain can be pulled and tied to this side. Tie it above center, as this clears more of the window to let light in. The curtain must slide along the rod to do this, so make sure it can move. Little rope loops will be fine. Also, make sure the curtain rod is smooth and round so the curtain can slide easily.

When you pull the curtain across the window at the end of the day, there will still be a space on the other side where air can get next to the window and cool down. If you want to keep in the most warmth with your curtain, you have to make a tight seal here too. This can be done simply, with a wood screw and a common lumber yard "furring strip." The furring strip holds the curtain against the window frame. This gives a good seal and you have only to pull the furring strip to one side to move the curtain.

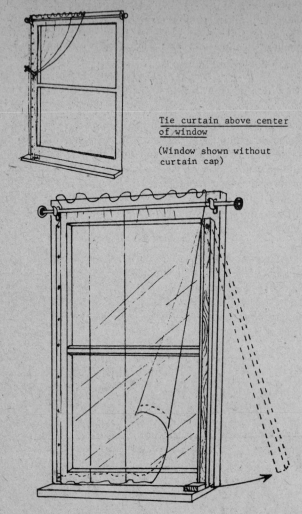

Tie curtain above center
of window

(Window shown without
curtain cap)

Strip swings out to release curtain

(Window shown without curtain cap)

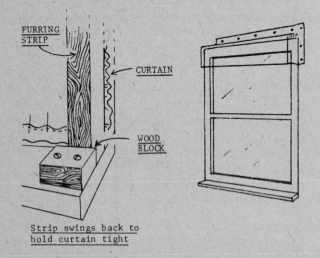

FURRING
STRIP

CURTAIN

WOOD
BLOCK

Strip swings back to
hold curtain tight

This kind of curtain will really reduce your heating bill. In summer, use it to trap heat at the window and help keep your house cool. Just pull down the top of the window a bit, and the closed curtain will let hot air back out of the window in summer.

Maintenance procedures for energy saving

Sealing Large Holes

The major reason for high heat bills is that cold air seeps into the house through cracks and holes. Whether the holes are large or small, they all rob you of heat.

Especially on windy days, leaks make the house very hard to heat. Cold drafts, particularly along the floor, can make you uncomfortable. If you have to pay for heat, leaks can cost you up to 20% of your heat bill! So let's "button up" for winter—keep warm and comfortable—and save lots of money as well.

Attic and Roof

Seal any openings between your attic and the rest of your house where air might escape, such as spaces around loosely-fitting attic stairway doors or pull-down stairways, penetrations of the ceiling for lights or a fan, and plumbing vents, pipes, or air ducts which pass into the attic—they don't seem like much, but they add up.

Check for broken or cracked glass. If the glass is broken, try to put a new piece in with putty. Be careful to remove the old glass with gloves or a cloth, so you don't cut yourself.

Sometimes it's easier to patch the glass if the hole is small or the glass is just cracked. "Freezer tape" criss-crossed over the hole or taped along the crack works just fine.

Look for holes in your roof and walls. One sure sign is the presence of water-marks on ceilings and walls. You should patch roof holes with tar paper or shingles. Walls can be patched with tar paper spread over "sealer", or mortar can be used on concrete and brick walls.

On the inside of your house, look for holes which let air go up through the ceiling. Make sure that the attic door closes tightly. Are there openings around pipes or flues which go up through the ceiling? All of these let heat escape.

You can use newspaper or cloth to seal around the edge of attic doors. Cloth is better for sealing around pipes. Stuff it into the hole. If there are holes around the place where

Remove broken glass with
gloves, cloth, or pliers

Add putty

Use glazier points to
hold glass, then putty

the chimney or flue goes through the ceiling stuff cloth in the hole and finish off with mortar.

Sealing Foundations and Floors

Many older houses develop air leaks through the floor. One problem is that heat escapes. Another problem is that cold air can blow in from below. Houses on poles and those with stone foundations let the wind blow underneath the floor. Here are some things you can do to keep Old Man Winter out:

Cover your floors with old rugs. If you don't have enough, these can be bought cheaply at garage sales and auctions. Before you lay the rug down, cover the floor with several layers of newspaper and then tack down the rug.

If the foundation around the house is open or has a space where the wind can get in, enclose it. This can be done by "banking." Fill old sacks with dirt or leaves and stuff these around the edge of the house to fill the space between the sill and the ground.

Basements

If you can't afford to insulate the exposed portions of your basement or crawl space for the winter, you can still create some barriers against wind and cold by planting shrubs around the foundation. You can also tar paper the exposed walls and rake leaves against the foundation, covering them with a weighted tarp (the tar paper keeps moisture off your house that would otherwise come in through the leaves).

Another way is to nail tar paper or plastic to the sill and drape it to the ground. Hold it in place with rocks, bricks, or dirt. Whichever way you do it, make good use of the snows when they come. Shovel snow over the sacks or tarpaper to fill in any air spaces. The snow also helps keep heat in.

FRONT VIEW

It's helpful to place a few sacks of
leaves beneath ends of tar-paper to
block the wind

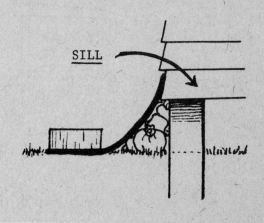

SILL

SIDE VIEW

Insulate Your Water Heater and Save Fuel

Now you can buy for your home water heater an insulation refit kit that can save both money and fuel. The kit consists of a blanket of fiberglass insulation and comes with do-it-yourself installation instructions. The additional insulation on the water heater reduces the rate of heat loss, which also reduces the energy required to keep the water at the desired temperature. Studies show that, on a national average, the use of the kit will save $5 to $20 per year on your utility bill and repay your initial investment (under $20) in energy savings within 15 months for electric water heaters and within 3½ years for gas water heaters. Also, a refit kit can be used safely on electric water heaters as well as on gas water heaters when installation instructions are followed carefully. *Extreme care must be exercised when installing the insulation of a gas water heater.*

How does more insulation help?

Just as a blanket or a coat helps maintain your body temperature, a storage tank protected by additional layers of insulation maintains water temperature better and longer.

The refit kit is designed for easy installation.

How can I get a well-insulated water heater?

When buying a new water heater, you have the opportunity to choose one with a well-insulated lining. This usually means selecting the one with the thickest available insulation. However, most homes already have a water heater. Refitting it with an outside layer of fiberglass insulation will improve its energy efficiency and save money on utility bills.

How much energy could I save a year using a refit kit?

With 1½ inches of additional insulation, heat loss can be cut by about 400 kilowatt hours per year for electric water heaters and by about 3600 cubic feet per year for gas water heaters.

Note: In lieu of purchasing a refit kit, you may find it more economical to buy blanket-type insulating material to wrap the tank of an electric water heater. Of course, use of the kit is more convenient and may result in a neater appearance. Buying blanket-type insulation material is NOT recommended for gas water heaters. For safety, use ONLY the refit kit if you have a gas water heater.

Use of Hot Water Heaters

Hot water heating, stoves, and refrigerators use up $1 out of every $5 that you spend for energy. Let's see if you can save some dollars here as well.

Don't overheat your water. Use the lowest temperature you can. Most people find that 110° to 120° is good. Turn down the thermostat on your water heater. There is a dial for this, usually near the pilot light. Turn it from a "High" or "Hot" setting to a "Low" or "Warm" setting.

Insulate the pipe between the hot water heater and the faucet. This helps keep the hot water in the pipe warm. Either pipe insulation or wraparound insulation is good for this. You can buy either at most hardware stores.

What else can I do to make household hot water use more energy-efficient?

— Lower the temperature setting on your heater to the lowest degree acceptable to your needs.
— Never leave hot water running unnecessarily.
— Fix leaky hot water faucets.
— Limit dishwasher runs to full loads.
— Consider installing a flow restrictor in the showerhead pipe to reduce water flow. Flow restrictors are available at most stores that handle plumbing supplies.
— Consider using faucet aerators. They mix air with water and reduce the amount of water used yet provide a water flow turbulent enough for washing.
— Launder clothes in cold or warm water whenever practical.
— Run full wash loads or adjust the water level control on your washer to the size of your washload.

Use as little hot water as you can for washing. For dishes, fill the basin or a small tub with warm soapy water once. Then wash. Rinse dishes with cold water. The same is true for washing hands and face, and shaving. Fill the basin once. Don't let the hot water run for washing. After washing dishes or bathing, leave the hot water in the sink or tub until it cools off. It will help heat the room, and put a little moisture into the air.

Fix leaky faucets. These waste both hot and cold water. They cost you money. Usually a drip can be stopped by replacing the washer.

Hot water

All your leaky faucets should be fixed—particularly the hot ones. One leaky faucet can waste up to 6000 gallons of water a year. You can also save by turning your water heater down when you'll be away from home for a weekend or more. Always use full loads in your dishwasher and clothes washer, and use warm wash and cold rinse. Take showers—they use less hot water than baths. You should use cold water to run your garbage disposal. In general, you *save* every time you use cold water instead of hot.

Kitchen, laundry and bath

Heating water is second only to heating and cooling residences in energy consumption. It accounts for 15 % of the energy used in the home and 3 % of all the energy used in the United States. Sensible use of hot water, along with conservative use of electricity, is the basis for the following tips:

in the kitchen . . .

Be sure the dishwasher is full, but not overloaded, before you turn it on. An average dishwasher uses 14 gallons of hot water per load. If every dishwasher used in the country cut out just one load a week, the country could save the equivalent of about 9,000 barrels of oil each day (enough to heat 140,000 homes in winter).

Scrape dishes before loading them in the washer. Rinsing is seldom necessary, but when it is, use cold water.

Let your dishes air dry. After the final rinse, turn off the control knob of the dishwasher and open the door.

Use proper defrosting methods for manual refrigerator/freezers. These appliances consume less energy than those that defrost automatically, but they must be defrosted frequently and as quickly as possible to maintain that edge. Frost should never be allowed to build up to more than one-quarter of an inch.

Most refrigerators have heating elements in their walls to prevent condensation on the outside. These heaters need only be turned on when the air is extremely humid. When buying such a refrigerator, be sure it has a switch to turn off the heaters. Better yet, buy one without heaters.

During holidays or other extended absences from home, empty the refrigerator, disconnect it from the power outlet, clean thoroughly, and leave the door ajar.

Check seals around the refrigerator and oven doors to make sure they are airtight. If not, adjust the latch or replace the seal.

Reduce energy consumption in cooking. Use flat bottom pans that cover the burner heating element. More heat enters the pot and less is lost to the surrounding air.

Clean heat reflector below the stove heating element—it will reflect the heat better.

Pressure cookers save energy by reducing cooking time.

When using the oven, make the most of the heat from that single source. Plan all-oven-cooked meals, or fill the oven with other foods that can be used at a later time with a bit of heating. Use small heaters, or small ovens, for small meals.

in the laundry . . .

Wash clothes in warm or cold water, rinse in cold. You'll save energy and money. Use hot water only if absolutely necessary.

If everyone washed clothes in warm or cold water, national fuel savings would amount to the equivalent of about 100,000 barrels of oil a day. That is, 2½% of the total demand for residential heating (enough to heat 1.6 million homes in winter).

Fill clothes washers (unless they have small-load attachments or variable water levels) and dryers, but do not overload them.

If every household cut the use of clothes washers and dryers by 25%, the Nation would save the equivalent of 35,000 barrels of oil per day (enough to heat over 400 billion gallons of water a day).

Remove clothes from the dryer as soon as they are dry. Extra running time is pure waste.

Separate drying loads into heavy and lightweight items. Since the lighter ones take less drying time, the dryer doesn't have to be on as long for these loads.

Dry your clothes in consecutive loads. The energy used to bring the dryer up to the desired temperature shouldn't be allowed to go to waste.
Keep the lint screen in the dryer clean by removing lint after each load.

in the bath . . .

Take more showers than tub baths. Showers use less hot water, hence less energy than tub baths.

Consider installing a flow restrictor in the pipe at the showerhead to restrict the flow to an adequate 4 gallons per minute. This is easy to do and can save considerable amounts of hot water and the energy used to produce it. The showerhead should unscrew easily, and flow restrictors are available at most plumbing supply stores. In areas where the water pressure remains fairly constant, a washer with a small hold inserted in the pipe should serve nicely.

Refrigerators

These are next in line for attention. Here are some things you can do to save dollars:

Turn the refrigerator to the warmest setting that will keep food from spoiling. There is a dial inside the refrigerator for this, and you can check the temperature with a thermometer. 40° is fine for the refrigerator, and 10° for the freezer.

Make sure the gasket on the refrigerator door closes tightly. To test for this, close the door on some newspaper. If the paper pulls out easily, you need a new gasket. Also, make sure that the door on the freezer closes correctly.

Open and close the refrigerator doors a little as possible. Don't let children play here.

Most foods should be cooled outside the refrigerator after cooking. A few recipes call for rapid chilling, but most things can be cooled in the house. This reduces the load on the refrigerator.

If the refrigerator is near a heater or a sunny window, move it to a cooler spot in the kitchen.

Cooking

When baking or broiling, try to use full oven capacity. Don't use the oven for very small quantities of food. A burner, though less efficient, will be more energy-efficient than heating up the whole oven for small quantities.

If possible, turn off the pilot lights on a gas stove. These eat up gas all the time, whether you are using the stove or not. A fourth of your cooking bill can be wasted on the pilot light! You can light the burners as you use them with kitchen matches or, better yet, a flint lighter. *Never blow the pilot light out!* Be sure the gas to the pilot light is "off," by shutting off its valve on the burner.

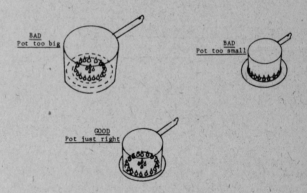

Use the oven rather than the burners when you can. Since the oven is insulated, it makes better use of its heat and costs less for cooking. Also, try to cook several foods at once in the oven. Choose foods that cook at nearly the same temperature. You can cook two or three things for little more than the cost of one this way.

When you use the burners, choose pans that have wide, flat bottoms that just cover the burner and absorb all the heat. When water is used in cooking, such as for vegetables, use just enough water to steam them and prevent sticking—and cover the pot with a lid. Don't overcook. This wastes energy and also food value.

Move Heat Away From the Heater!

Try to get more heat out into the room where it can be used. Don't let it get trapped behind or above radiators and heaters.

Keep heat away from the walls behind radiators and wood stoves. This can be done with reflectors made of thin sheet metal which direct the heat out into the room. Aluminum foil glued to cardboard will do fine, too. Make sure cardboard is at least six inches away from touching the radiator or wood stove, though. Feel it to make sure it's not getting too hot and move it farther away if you have to. Direct the heat away from the ceiling and into the room.

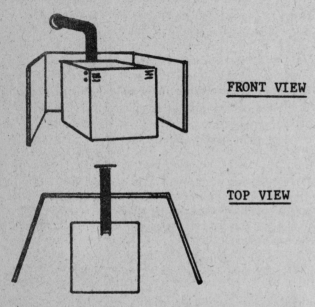

FRONT VIEW

TOP VIEW

You can make this stove reflector easily

Radiators are usually placed by windows so that they heat the cold air around them. This heat rises to the ceiling where it is of little use. Make a reflector. By curving the metal at the top, you can direct some of this warm air into the room. With a cardboard and aluminum foil reflector, bend the cardboard in towards the room a few inches from the top of the reflector.

Remember: Heat the house only when you're home. Close off doors, windows, and rooms which you don't use. If some parts of the house are cold, move heat from warm rooms and away from radiators and stoves to heat the cold areas. Doing these things will make your house more comfortable. It will also save you some more money, maybe another $10 or $15 of each $100 you usually spend for heat.

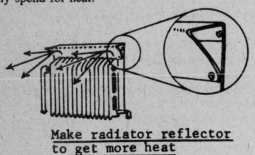

Make radiator reflector
to get more heat

Electricity—The energy that comes to us from generators

If everyone scheduled household chores so as to lighten the load at the generating plants during peak hours, fewer inefficient generating units would have to be placed in service, and the utilities' daily fuel consumption would be reduced. So would the possibilities of brownouts and blackouts.

Lights

Plan your lighting sensibly. Reduce lighting were possible, concentrating it in work areas or reading areas where it is really needed. Fluorescent bulbs should be used rather than the incandescent kind.

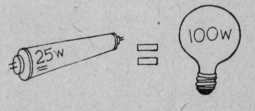

A 25-watt fluorescent bulb gives off as much light as a 100-watt incandescent bulb, but costs one fourth as much to light. Decorative gas lanterns should be turned off or converted to electric lamps. They will use much less energy to produce the same amount of light.

Careful use of lighting provides the homemaker other conservation opportunities. To save electricity through wise lighting:
Remove one bulb out of three and replace it with a burned-out bulb for safety; replace others with bulbs of the next lower wattage. But be sure to provide adequate lighting for safety (e.g., in stairwells). Concentrate light in reading and working areas, and for safety.

This should save about 4% in electricity costs in the average home.

Turn off all lights when not needed. [One 100-watt bulb burning for 10 hours uses 11,600 Btu's, or the equivalent of a pound of coal or one-half pint of oil.]

Use fluorescent lights in suitable areas—on the desk, in the kitchen and bath, among others. They give more lumens per watt. One 40-watt fluorescent tube, for example, provides more light than three 60-watt incandescent bulbs. (A 40-watt fluorescent lamp gives off about 80 lumens per watt; a 60-watt incandescent gives off only 14.7 lumens per watt. The lower-watt but higher-lumen fluorescent would save about 140 watts of electricity over a period of 7 hours.)

PART 7: FIREPLACES AND HEATING STOVES

The Fireplace Plug

Want to enjoy and use your fireplace during the winter season without awakening the next morning to a cold house? The "morning after" chill develops after the fire dies and the fireplace with its open damper changes from a source of heat to a monster that draws warm air very effectively from the room and up the chimney flue — and keeps the furnace operating and running up your fuel bills.

Now the problem is solved. As soon as the fire dies down, or when the family is ready for bed, put an *operculum* against the fireplace opening. The first to use an *operculum* was the Marquis Roland de Roberge in his chateau with its twenty fireplaces.

It's best to use heavy-gauge, galvanized steel. Your *operculum* (or fireplace lid) should be large enough to extend over the opening so that it covers a portion of the surrounding brick. On the steel lid, the edges of sides and top are bent inward for a close fit against the brick. A handle is set on the front and steel shelf brackets serve as feet. The entire *operculum* front can be painted with black, heat-resistant paint. In addition to making it possible to enjoy one's fireplace, no matter what the weather, the "Roberge" *operculum* also provides safety. When a blazing fire is left, set the fireplace plug in place and no sparks can fly out while the room is unattended.

Both fireplaces and stoves can be used for heating the whole house, or you can use them for extra heat. When you have a choice between a fireplace and a stove, use the stove. Stoves give off more heat. If there are two chimneys in the house, use the one on the inside wall. It will draw better and give more heat, too.

Close the damper when the stove or fireplace is not in use. Be sure the fire is *completely* out! Leaving the damper open will waste a lot of heat. There are a couple of things you can do if your heater doesn't have a damper. On stoves, you can buy at many hardware stores a special section of stovepipe with a damper in it. If you have a fireplace, stuff a newspaper a little way up the flue. Pull the paper down and use it to start the next fire.

Fireplaces use a lot of air to keep the fire going. Fresh cold air will seep in around doors and windows to replace what goes out the flue. So a fireplace can even cool your house down! For the greatest comfort, close some doors and try to draw air in through empty rooms. *Don't* build a roaring fire. These waste fuel because the heat goes up the chimney before you can use it. Burn wood and coals *slowly*.

Fireplaces

Many folks use fireplaces for extra heat. Usually a lot of wood has to be burned because fireplaces are not very efficient. This happens for two reasons. First, even small fires draw large amounts of cold air into the house to feed the fire. This creates cold drafts along the floor and cools the house. Second, as soon as the heat comes off the fire, it is drawn up the flue. Not much heat gets out into the room.

Because of these problems, you have to cut or purchase a lot of firewood. You won't get very much heat for all your work. The two projects outlined here, however, will help solve these problems. If you put them both to work for you, it's possible to almost double the heat you get from your fireplace!

Fireplace Air Vent

Put a vent under your floor to feed air to the fireplace. This will reduce the amount of air which is drawn across the room from cracks around windows and doors.

The easiest way to connect a vent to the outside is to use a series of rectangular metal ducts. You can get these ducts at a plumbing supply store. Different sizes are available, but try to buy ducts which are at least 3" deep by 10" wide. You will need enough to stretch under your floor from just in front of the fireplace to the *nearest* opening in the basement.

Now, cut a hole for one end of the duct system right in front of the fireplace. Then make an opening in the basement wall or through a basement window for another duct to go through to the outside. When you put the basement duct in place, tilt it down a little toward the out-of-doors. This will allow any moisture to drain out.

Two elbows are attached to the duct system. One should be placed face down with a screen covering it, just outside

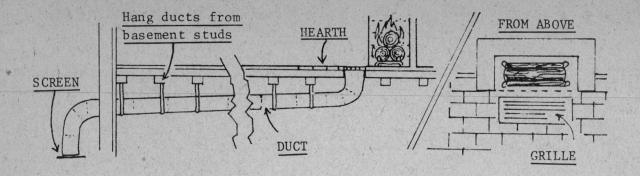

SCREEN

Hang ducts from basement studs

HEARTH

DUCT

FROM ABOVE

GRILLE

the house where the basement duct comes through. This will keep the rain, wind, leaves, and insects out of the duct. The other is used where the fireplace duct comes through the floor just in front of the fireplace.

Once you have the ducts in place, you finish the job by placing a grille over the opening in the floor. Use a strong grille so you can walk on it, and try to get one which can be closed. When the fireplace is not in use, close the grille and put a throw rug over it.

Fireplace Air Heater

The next step is to capture more of the fire's heat before it goes up the flue. There is an easy way to do this. Build a fireplace air heater which not only holds the burning wood but also forces warm air out into the room.

The heater is made of 1-inch iron pipes bent into a sort of "C" shape. The vertical pieces are bent around so that the top of the pipes extends just outside the fireplace.

Pipe elbows can be used to make the connection between these vertical pieces and the bottom pipe sections of the heater. Make the bottom pieces just long enough to come out in front of the mantel a few inches, but stay behind your new air vent grille.

Make enough of these "C"-shaped pipes to come all the way across the face of your fireplace, with a 3-inch or 4-inch space between each "C." The "C's" rest on and are attached to a base made of iron pipe also. The legs of

the base should be 2" to 3" high and can be made by bending each end of the pipe. Have the "C"-shaped pipes welded to the base at a local welding shop. The cost should only be a few dollars.

This air heater works by sucking cold air from the floor. The air is heated by the fire, and then flows out into the room. It is possible to couple a fan along the front of the "C"-shaped pipes in order to increase the cold air supply and thereby increase the warm air circulation.

Install a wood burning stove

Adding a small stove can be a low-cost way of getting some extra heat. Wood and coal stoves, some in really great condition, can be bought cheaply at garage sales and auctions. Generally, it is worthwhile to purchase the good air-tight stoves as they hold a fire, are efficient, and do not create a fire hazard. Cover the rug or floor under your new stove with an asbestos sheet, and place tin or aluminum on top of the asbestos. This reflects heat up and keeps the floor cooler. Floor covering should be at least ¼" asbestos millboard covered with sheet metal. Cover floor 12" around sides and rear and 18" in front.

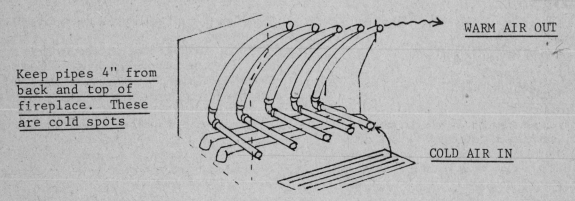

Keep pipes 4" from back and top of fireplace. These are cold spots

WARM AIR OUT

COLD AIR IN

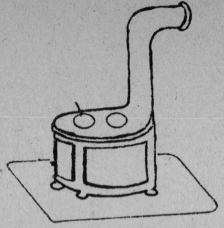

There are certain procedures you should follow to make sure the installation is safe!

The suggestions included herein are minimal safety procedures. You should contact your local authority (fire department or building inspector) for any special requirements or building restrictions.

These simple rules will help:

DO—Make sure of proper clearances from combustible floors, walls and ceilings.

DO—Have the chimney inspected by a competent mason.

DO—Check the condition frequently for signs of deterioration.

DO—Use a metal container to dispose of ashes outside the home.

DO—Install a smoke detector and fire extinguisher.

DO—Use, dry, well-seasoned wood. Burning green wood results in dirty chimneys.

DO—Be sure to check your city or county fire and safety codes. Also, inform your home insurance company of the installation of a fireplace.

DON'T—Extend pipe through walls or ceilings if at all possible.

DON'T—Connect a wood stove to a fireplace chimney unless the fireplace has been sealed off.

DON'T—Use flammable fuels to ignite wood. Use paper or kindling.

DON'T burn pine or other wood which develops pitch or other tar-like residue.

DON'T—add an extra flue to your chimney without checking with your local fire department or building official.

A disaster may cut off your normal source of heat for hours or days. If the weather is severe you may face a crisis. You need heat for your personal safety and comfort and to prevent freezing of the water lines in your home. This publication gives guidelines for setting up coal- or wood-burning stoves and fireplaces. The effort and expense in preparing for such an emergency could have great returns.

Some Supplies You Will Need

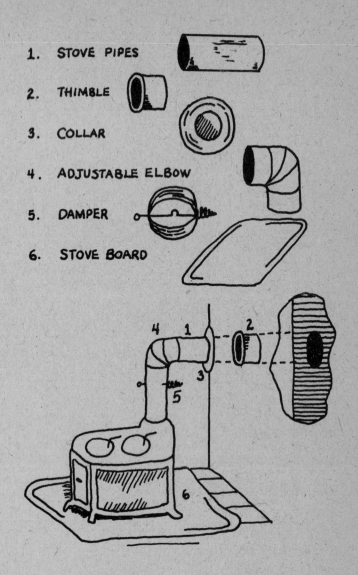

1. STOVE PIPES
2. THIMBLE
3. COLLAR
4. ADJUSTABLE ELBOW
5. DAMPER
6. STOVE BOARD

Setting Up a Stove in a Fireplace

1. Measure fireplace and cut a sheet of metal or asbestos board to close the opening.
2. Set stove on a fireproof stove board at least one stove pipe length (24'') away from the face of the fireplace.
3. Install a damper in one section of the pipe.
4. Connect pipes to stove and elbow and adjust to determine proper location of hole in sheet metal or asbestos board.
5. Slide collar on pipe and insert pipe into the hole in closing board. Then fit the collar snugly against the board.

Caution: Burn coal only in a cast iron stove with a grate designed specifically for coal.

SPECIFIC PROCEDURE FOR INSTALLATION OF WOOD BURNING STOVES

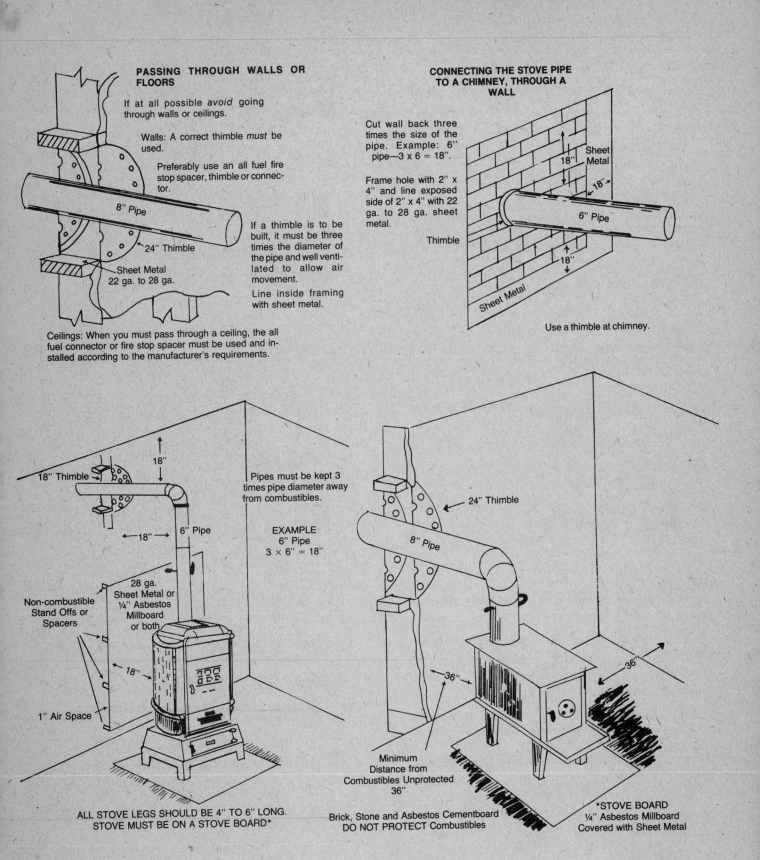

PASSING THROUGH WALLS OR FLOORS

If at all possible *avoid* going through walls or ceilings.

Walls: A correct thimble *must* be used.

Preferably use an all fuel fire stop spacer, thimble or connector.

8" Pipe

24" Thimble

Sheet Metal 22 ga. to 28 ga.

If a thimble is to be built, it must be three times the diameter of the pipe and well ventilated to allow air movement.

Line inside framing with sheet metal.

Ceilings: When you must pass through a ceiling, the all fuel connector or fire stop spacer must be used and installed according to the manufacturer's requirements.

CONNECTING THE STOVE PIPE TO A CHIMNEY, THROUGH A WALL

Cut wall back three times the size of the pipe. Example: 6" pipe—3 x 6 = 18".

Frame hole with 2" x 4" and line exposed side of 2" x 4" with 22 ga. to 28 ga. sheet metal.

Thimble

18"

Sheet Metal

18"

6" Pipe

18"

Sheet Metal

Use a thimble at chimney.

18" Thimble

18"

18"

6" Pipe

Pipes must be kept 3 times pipe diameter away from combustibles.

EXAMPLE
6" Pipe
3 × 6" = 18"

Non-combustible Stand Offs or Spacers

28 ga. Sheet Metal or ¼" Asbestos Millboard or both

18"

1" Air Space

ALL STOVE LEGS SHOULD BE 4" TO 6" LONG. STOVE MUST BE ON A STOVE BOARD*

24" Thimble

8" Pipe

36"

36"

Minimum Distance from Combustibles Unprotected 36"

Brick, Stone and Asbestos Cementboard DO NOT PROTECT Combustibles

*STOVE BOARD ¼" Asbestos Millboard Covered with Sheet Metal

Free Standing Stove or Fireplace

1. Set stove on fireproof foundation (asbestos-metal stove board, brick, marble, chips, etc.).
2. Install a prefabricated, insulated metal chimney, approved by the Underwriter's Laboratories (UL).
3. Prefabricated chimneys are available for use through a roof or an outside wall and can be installed in mobile homes.

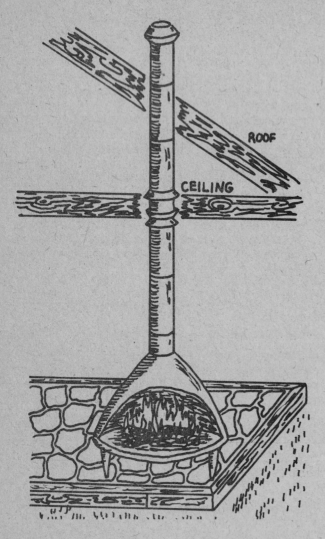

Fuel your stove

You can burn just about anything in "chunk stoves." You can burn paper, logs, small chunks of wood, broken-up wooden boxes, or coal. A nice way to make use of extra newspaper or magazines is to make paper logs. Roll up the paper in round log-like shapes, tie these with string, and let them soak in water until fully wet. Dry them out near a heat source. The moisture helps fight winter dryness in the house. Once dry, paper logs burn almost like wood and keep a good fire going for quite some time.

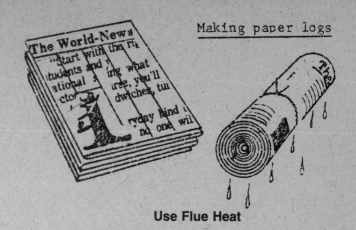

Making paper logs

Use Flue Heat

On both furnaces and heating stoves much of the heat goes up the flue and is wasted. You can take some of this back by putting metal "donut rings" on the flue. These give off heat.

The easiest and least expensive metal to work with is aluminum. You can buy "aluminum flashing" or "aluminum grass edging" at a hardware store. Get one roll of it.

Get all the heat you can from the fuel you burn! Keep your heating system in top shape and burn the fuel carefully and slowly. You can save another $10 out of each $100 you usually spend for heat.

The donuts in place on the flue

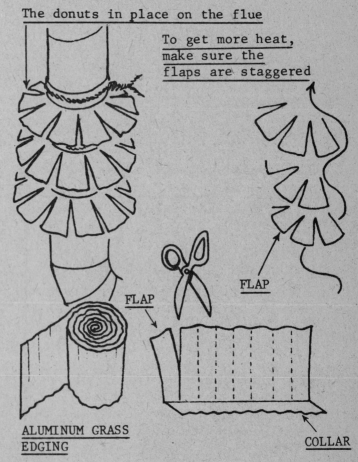

To get more heat, make sure the flaps are staggered

Heating with Wood

Increasing costs and, in some cases, current or projected shortages of other fuels have increased interest in the use of wood as a heating fuel. The manufacturers of wood burning units have responded to the new interest in fuelwood with improved construction and efficiency in their combustion units.

Fuelwood is either sold by weight, the load, or the stack. There are various sized stacks and confusion often exists over the amount of wood in a "cord." A standard cord of wood is defined by law as a pile 4' high and 8' long made up of sticks 4' in length. A "face cord" is a pile 4' x 8' made up of sticks of any length (often either 12", 16", or 20"). The amount of solid wood in the stack depends upon the size and straightness of the sticks and whether they are round or split. Thus, a standard cord may contain from 60 to 110 cubic feet of solid wood.

Wood dealers often eliminate the need to define a cord by selling wood by the load or by weight. Of course, the amount of wood in a "truck load" depends upon the type of vehicle.

Fuelwood Preparation

Some of the other factors that should be considered when preparing wood for burning are:

Cutting — Should be done at least six to nine months prior to burning. It often requires a chain saw which is perhaps the most hazardous operation connected with preparing wood. Keeping the leaves on summer-cut trees until they wither helps remove a great deal of moisture from the wood.

Splitting — Greatly reduces drying time. It is often necessary for efficient handling and combustion and is best done when wood is frozen or green.

Stacking — Necessary for proper drying of the wood and should be done immediately after splitting. Cover and allow for adequate air circulation.

Seasoning — Necessary to reduce moisture content of the wood and assure proper combustion.

How Wood Burns

Wood burns in three phases — (1) Heat drives water from the wood. (This heat does not warm the stove or the room.) (2) Charcoal and volatile gases are formed. The gases can produce 50 to 60 percent of the heat value of the wood; but they must be heated to about 1100 °F and mixed with sufficient oxygen to burn. (3) Following the release of the volatile gases, the charcoal burns. These phases overlap so that all occur at the same time.

Fuelwood Characteristics

The heat derived from the combustion of wood depends upon the concentration of woody materials, resins, ash and water. In general, the heaviest woods (hickories, oaks, locust), when seasoned, have the greatest heating value per cord. Lighter woods (aspen, basswood, willow) give about the same heat value per pound but they give less heat per cord because they are less dense. When considering the type of wood to burn, other important characteristics are:

—ease of splitting (apple, birch, maple, oak)
—ease of ignition (birch, cedar, pine)
—production of heavy smoke (cedar, spruce)
—sparking (cedar, hemlock)
—coaling qualities (apple, cherry, hickory, maple, oak)

The use of wood for home heating has several disadvantages. Fuelwood must be well-seasoned (dried) in order to be most efficient.

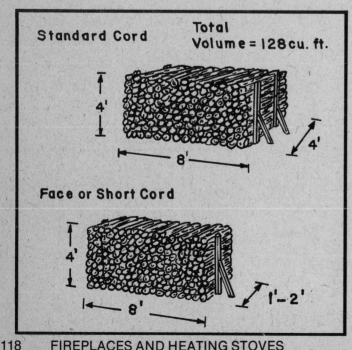

Standard Cord — Total Volume = 128 cu. ft. — 4' / 8' / 4'

Face or Short Cord — 4' / 8' / 1'–2'

Variation of Heating Values of Wood Due to Moisture	
Percent of Moisture	Percent of Usable Heat
0 (oven dry)	103.4
4	102.7
10	101.6
20 (air-dried hard wood)	100 (7,250 Btu)*
40	96.5
80	89.7
100	85.00

*Btu is the quantity of heat required to raise the temperature of one pound of water one degree Fahrenheit.

As a fuel, wood burns rapidly so that refueling must be frequent. Also, it is heavy and hard to transport.

Although the production of fuelwood is a rather dirty business, wood is a relatively clean fuel producing about 1 percent ash by weight. Wood heat produces relatively small amounts of chemical air pollution. But the production of particles in the air tends to be higher than with other conventional fuels.

A disadvantage in heating with wood is the high fire hazard. To prevent the possibility of fire outside the heating unit, the wood should be burned in sound, well-constructed stoves or fireplaces. Stoves should have dampers to control the rate of burning. The chimney must be sound with all joints properly mortared. When constructing new chimneys, use earthen flue tile to prevent super-heated gasses from escaping between the bricks to flammable materials.

Heat Values

Generally, heat values are dependent on the percent of moisture and the weight of the wood. Heavier woods have a higher heat value. The heat value from an air-dried standard cord of several native hardwoods (such as hickory and oak) when burned in a modern efficient woodburning unit is equal to nearly 130 gallons of No. 2 fuel oil.

Burning characteristics vary with wood species. Elm tends to burn slowly with little or no flame while white birch and pine burn quickly with much crackling and spark-throwing. Green wood is not efficiently burned in ordinary stoves.

The lighting or kindling of a fire in a stove or fireplace is dependent upon heating the wood to the point of ignition or the kindling point. Some woods also have a low kindling point, such as small pieces of dry white pine; pieces of white birch bark or softwood cones can be used to ignite woods that are more difficult to burn. Also, paper and cardboard are good kindling materials. Highly flammable liquids such as gasoline should NEVER be used to kindle fires.

Approximate Weight and Heating Value per Cord (80 cu. ft.) of Different Air-Dried Woods

Woods	Weight, lb. Air dry	Available heat, Millions Btu	Equivalent in gallons of fuel oil
Ash	3440	20.01	145
Aspen	2160	12.5	91
Beech, American	3760	21.8	158
Birch, Yellow	3680	21.3	154
Elm, American	2900	17.2	125
Hickory, shagbark	4240	24.6	178
Maple, red	3200	18.6	135
Maple, sugar	3680	21.3	154
Oak, red	3680	21.3	154
Oak, white	3920	22.7	165
Pine, eastern white	2080	13.3	96

Chimney Construction

Chimneys are constructed of either masonry or prefabricated metal. The metal chimneys have concentric walls with air spaces or insulation in between. The chimneys should have the label ALL FUEL from a recognized testing lab such as Underwriter's Laboratories (UL). Masonry chimneys may be brick, cinder block, or stone. Tile flue liners are standard for masonry chimneys. Older chimneys often have no tile lining so check them carefully for leaks. It is best to locate the chimney on an interior wall to maintain higher flue temperatures and thus to reduce the formation of creosote. The figure illustrates one approved method for connecting the stove pipe to the chimney. The cost of metal pre-fab versus masonry chimneys depends a great deal upon the individual installation method used. Masonry chimneys usually have the longest life. Pre-fab chimneys with a stainless steel inner and outer lining have a longer life than those of galvanized sheet steel.

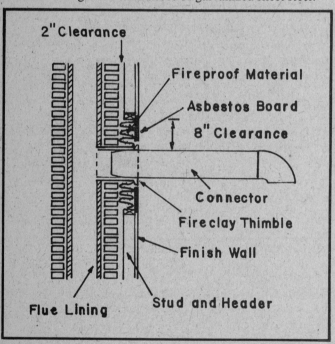

Multiflues

Do not connect a wood stove to the same flue serving a fireplace because sparks and flue gases from the stove may enter the house through the open fireplace.

Room heaters, cook stoves, etc. should not be connected to a common flue because (1) flue gases and sparks may pass from one flue opening to another and (2) multiple connections sometimes cause a poor draft and unsatisfactory operation. If, despite these recommendations, two stoves are connected to the same chimney, the connections must enter the chimney at different elevations.

Wood Stove Safety— The Creosote Problem

Creosote is found almost anywhere in a wood heating system, from the top of the chimney to the inside of the stove itself. It is caused by unburned gasses found in wood smoke which condense on cool surfaces.

The form which creosote takes depends on the temperature of the surface on which it condenses. For example, if it condenses on a relatively cool surface, such as an exterior stovepipe, the creosote will contain much water and will be very fluid. It may even be seen dripping from the joints of the stove-pipe.

Creosote-clogged Pipe and Flue

Creosote Dripping From Flue

When there is condensation on a surface of 150 degrees F. or more, a smaller amount of water is present and the creosote will be very thick, sticky and similar to tar. This form is particularly hard to remove from surfaces. Whatever form creosote takes, it is always dark brown or black and has a very unpleasant, acrid odor.

Hard to Remove

If allowed to remain in the chimney or pipe, the form of creosote will continue to change. The longer it is heated, the more water will evaporate, until finally the creosote takes the form of carbon. In this form it is flaky and shiny on one side and may be brushed or scraped off. Other forms are difficult to remove even with a stiff wire brush.

Creosote-clogged Pipe

Many factors influence creosote buildup. Probably the most commonly-discussed factor is related to the type of wood burned and its moisture content. Dry hardwoods are generally assumed to generate the least amount of creosote but the quantity can still be large. Creosote formation is not entirely eliminated no matter what kind of wood is burned.

Dry Wood

The amount of creosote deposited depends mostly on (1) the density of the smoke and vapor from the fire (the less smoke, the less creosote), and (2) the temperature of the surface on which it is condensing (the higher the temperature, the less creosote).

Smoke Density Factor

Creosote generation is highest during low, smoldering burns. Smoke densities are least when combustion is relatively complete. This tends to be the case when the amount of air admitted to a wood burner is high. For this reason, leaky stoves, open stoves and fireplaces usually have fewer creosote problems than other wood-burning devices.

Stove Air Inlet

Smoke density can be lowered somewhat in an air-tight stove by using small amounts of wood and stoking more often or by using larger pieces of wood.

Creosote formation can be limited by leaving the air inlet slightly open after adding wood to promote more rapid burning until the wood is mostly reduced to charcoal. Then close the inlet as much as desired. This causes more complete combustion and burns the potential creosote-forming gasses. An additional amount of heat will be generated while the gasses are burning. This is a house-warming bonus.

Can Cause Chimney Fires

Because creosote forms more quickly on cooler surfaces, a well-insulated pre-fabricated metal chimney has the least serious creosote problem. The insulation helps keep the temperatures of the inner surfaces higher and the chimney's low heat capacity lets it warm up more rapidly after a fire is started. Flue temperatures can be increased by using a shorter stove pipe to connect the stove to the chimney. However, this decreases the energy efficiency of the system.

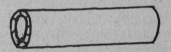

Insulated Stove Pipe

Creosote can burn and cause potentially-dangerous chimney fires. If a fire starts, the amount of air entering the stove should be decreased as much as possible.

Creosote, because of its acidity, causes corrosion in many materials, including steel and mortar. Masonry chimneys with tile liners or pre-fabricated insulated chimneys with stainless steel liners are corrosion-resistant. When properly installed, both types are also safer than non-lined chimneys in the event of a chimney fire. Chimneys without liners which are poorly-maintained are hazardous.

Keep Chimney Clean

In summary, to lessen the formation of creosote:

1. Keep the chimney clean. Check the need for cleaning before starting a fire in the fall. Then check after two weeks, one month, two months, etc., until you can determine how frequently your chimney should be cleaned.
2. When you are sure that your chimney is safe and clean, run a hot fire at least once each day, preferably in the morning while there is someone available to watch it.
3. Burn dry hardwood when possible.
4. Leave the air inlet slightly open after adding wood to promote more rapid burning until the wood is mostly reduced to charcoal. Then close the inlet as much as desired.
5. Use small amounts of wood and stoke more often or use larger pieces of wood.

PART 8: HOME HEATING IN AN EMERGENCY

At some time a situation may develop in which you might face a heating emergency—when your home heating system is inoperative for hours or days. At the critical time you must decide how to meet the emergency, either with an alternative source of heat or by seeking shelter elsewhere. Serious planning and preparation should be considered.

Safety is of prime importance in choosing an alternate form of heat. Consider all potential hazards and eliminate as many as possible, keeping in mind that your degree of protection is lower during a community emergency. Normal community services such as police and fire protection, doctors, hospitals, and highway maintenance may be in great demand and unable to respond to your emergency immediately. Under emergency conditions you may have to do certain things you wouldn't consider doing under normal circumstances. Use extreme caution.

PREPARING FOR AN EMERGENCY

The first step in making a plan is to determine the conditions your family might face if your heating system fails. Because all members of your family would be affected, each should have a hand in the planning. Try the following:

Discuss with your family what you might do if the heating system went off and were to remain off for several days and nights.

If your home is heated electrically, failure would obviously be caused by lack of power. But don't forget that most other systems depend on electricity, too. Oil burners usually have electrically-powered fuel injectors and ignition. Hot-air systems rely on a fan for air circulation; hot-water systems with zone valves and circulator pumps, or coal furnaces with motorized stokers, also need electricity. Most thermostats require electric power to operate.

Imagine that your area is experiencing an intense storm. It is cold and telephone service is disrupted. Then, with a pencil and pad handy, discuss how you would cope with the crisis. The family would have to determine what could be done to provide home heat, or at least how to keep members of the family warm. Discuss sources of alternate fuels available; how to get them and how to use them; what protective measures would be necessary such as keeping pipes from freezing; and supplying water if the pump is not operating. As part of the discussion you probably will want to draw up a list of additional obstacles that might be encountered, the responsibilities of each family member, and supplies available.

WHERE DO I BEGIN MY PLANNING?

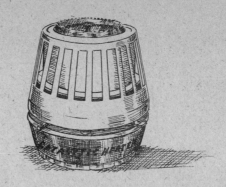

First, consider the resources you now have in your home for meeting emergencies. Because no two homes are the same, each homeowner must assess his own situation and prepare accordingly. Keep that pencil and paper handy!

YOUR RESOURCES

A. Could your heating system, with simple modification or through manual operation, continue to heat all or part of your home?

B. What other heating devices are used or stored in your home, garage, or barn? List them. Some suggestions:
   Fireplace
   Charcoal grill
   Wood, coal, gas, or oil stove or space heater
   Camping stove or heater
   Electric or gas oven and surface heating units
   Portable gas oven
   Gas-fired hot water heater
   Portable electric heater

C. List fuels available in your home or within reasonable distance. Which of them could be used in the above list of devices?
   Oil or kerosene
   Furnace, stove, or cannel coal
   Firewood, lumber, scraps, corncobs, straw
   Gas, campstove fuel, charcoal, starter fluid, alcohol, gasoline, motor oil
   Newspapers, magazines

If your heating device and fuel can be matched, would they provide enough heat to warm at least one room in your home? Is there enough fuel for several days? Do you have a secondary source of emergency heat?

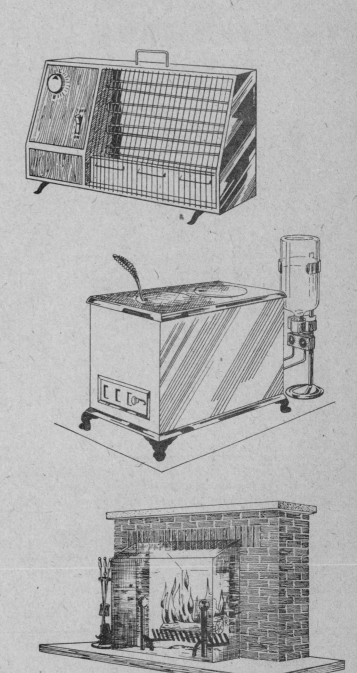

DECIDE NOW

If your regular heating system cannot be modified for an emergency, consider buying, building, or adapting a device or system that will. The choice might be a space heater, castiron or sheet-metal stove, or a catalytic heater. A small generator might be the answer if it will keep your furnace in operation. Your supplier or County Agent can help you decide what capacity generator you need. Perhaps you have been looking for an excuse to finally build that fireplace you've always wanted. Try to avoid depending on the same fuel for emergency heat as you have in your normal heating system.

PREPARATION

Now that you have decided how to heat your home during an emergency, it is time to get busy making preparations. Good planning now will give your family the confidence it needs when an emergency arises.

You will probably have to make some changes in your home or in your heating system to accommodate another heating device. If you can't make them, call in someone who can. Any device which burns fuel must be vented outside the house— both to eliminate smoke and gas and to provide oxygen for combustion.

ALTERING YOUR REGULAR HEATING SYSTEM

Minor alterations to your regular heating system might be considered:

A. Because automatic heating systems are often dependent upon electricity, you might wish to consider an emergency generator to provide power for full operation. This applies only to fossil-fueled systems with pumps, blowers, circulators, fuel injectors, electric ignition and thermostats. Electrically operated valves in many steam or hot air systems can often be operated manually. Hot air systems, depending on installation, are capable of providing limited heat without a blower. A coal-burning furnace can be fired the old fashioned way—with a shovel. Most small electrical generators such as might be available to the homeowner can supply only very limited power, inadequate for heating in an electrically heated home.

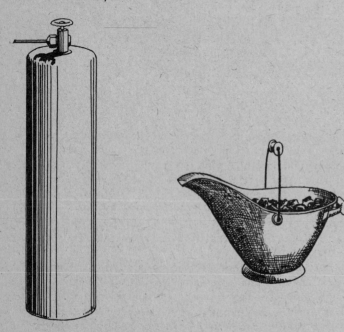

B. Sometimes another type of fuel can be burned in a heating system, for example wood can be used in a coal furnace. Get to know the capabilities and options of your primary heating system. If it can function at least partially in an emergency, it is your best source of heat.

PROVIDING VENTS AND FLUES

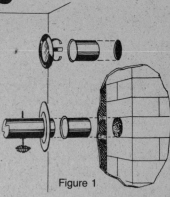

Figure 1

A. Install a "thimble," (a metal pipe which is inserted through the side of the chimney into the flue) to allow hooking up of a stove or space heater (See figure 1). If the heating device will be connected only during an emergency, fit the thimble with a metal or asbestos cap to cover the hole.

Note: chimney flues are designed to accommodate a single heating device at a time. Using more than one heating device at the same time on the same flue passage may result in smoke damage and improper burning of the fuel. If your auxiliary heating unit is to remain attached to the flue being used by the furnace, fireplace, or other burner, it should be fitted with a damper which will close off the device. Gas flues, which are usually smaller and lighter, cannot safely accommodate oil, coal, or wood burners. Gas devices, however, can be hooked to oil, coal, or wood flues.

Figure 2

B. Fireplaces in some homes are designed for appearance, not for their heat producing ability. If yours doesn't heat well, plug the throat with a piece of sheet metal with a hole cut for a stovepipe (See figure 2). In an emergency, a stove or heater can be set on the hearth. Stoves are better, more efficient heat producers than fireplaces.

C. Conventional masonry fireplaces are often not efficient producers of heat and may take more heat from a room than they put in. Heat circulating or "heatilator" fireplaces are much more efficient. Their ease of installation may offset their initial higher cost when compared with construction of conventional masonry fireplaces. Also, a glass-doored, heat circulating fireplace with special outside air inlets makes a satisfactory heater that can use wood, coal, and other combustibles.

D. If your present chimney cannot be used with an auxiliary heating system, consider installing a prefabricated chimney for use with your alternate source of heat.

USING OTHER FUELS

A. If oil is your emergency heating fuel and you have an oil fired furnace, install a drain cock or valve in the fuel line to draw oil from the tank. A siphon hose might be used if the tank has an access plug.

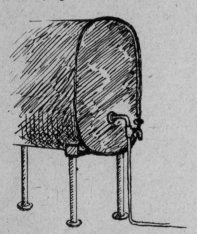

B. An emergency generator to keep your heating system functioning will involve special wiring for the changeover from utility power. Have an electrician advise you on this.

C. If gas is the standby fuel, be sure to have proper fittings, tubing, and tools on hand for a quick, safe hookup or changeover. Be sure that before placing any valve on your oil line that it is approved by your local building authority. Consult your fuel supplier on this change.

D. Heat pumps, units similar to air conditioners, can supply considerable amounts of heat under certain conditions. They may be practical for your situation as a source of heat which requires only electricity.

There is considerable heat in well water, which is usually at least 50 degrees F., in the northern States. Depending on the depth of water, this may be an efficient source of heat. The heat pump removes heat from the water and transfers it to the home. In warmer areas heat can be removed from outside air. Your local heating or air conditioning contractor can help you decide if a heat pump is practical for your situation.

GENERATORS FOR EMERGENCY POWER

An electric generator could supply power to run furnace blowers and oil burners and some other appliances in time of emergency. Just how many appliances you could operate depends on the output of the generator. Before buying a generator, the homeowner should add up the wattage required. Motor requirements should be figured at their starting rate (much higher than the running rate) to arrive at the total number of watts required at peak use. Generators are rated according to tneir kilowatt output (a kilowatt equals 1,000 watts).

Additional costs would be necessary to rewire the home service entrance, to install a transfer switch, or to add an alarm device or other accessories as desired, and for regular maintenance of the standby system. Home generators are usually driven either by an attached gasoline or gas-powered engine or a portable power source such as a tractor. The best information on a generating system for your home can be obtained from a local supplier, your utility company, or your County Agent or civil preparedness representative.

CONSERVING HEAT

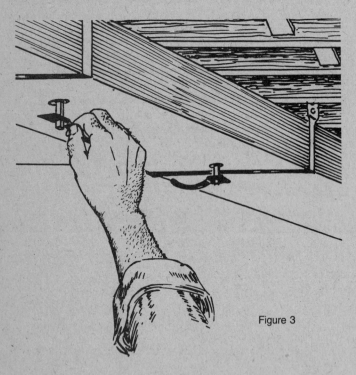

Figure 3

1. What other materials exist that could be used for conserving body warmth or emergency heat? Winter clothing, especially bulky items and outdoor garments, sleeping bags and small tents, blankets and bedding, drapes, curtains, slipcovers, rugs, large towels, etc., should be considered.

   Remember, if all else fails (and you can't get to other shelter) bed is the warmest place to be, with other family members and lots of covering.

2. How much of your house should you attempt to heat? When the heat goes off and you are going to have to rough it, the smaller the space you heat the easier the job will be. What you do will be dictated by the amount of emergency heat you have available, the floor plan of your house, and the severity of the cold outside. If you will be utilizing your fireplace or a stove requiring a chimney flue, the choice of rooms has been made for you. If, however, you will be able to obtain some heat from your furnace, select an area near it to cut down on heat loss that occurs in long pipe or duct runs. If you plan to use a portable heating device or have a choice among several heating zones, select an area on the "warm" side of the house away from prevailing cold winds. This area should have good insulation, as few windows as possible to minimize heat loss and should be capable of being isolated from other unheated areas either by closing doors or blocking openings to prevent drafts and heat loss. You may want to hang blankets or heavy drapes over windows to further reduce heat loss.

If you will be using your furnace in an emergency, know in advance how to prevent it from sending heat to unnecessary areas. In addition to shutting off the thermostat, this may involve blocking hot air ducts or shutting off certain steam or hot water lines (See figure 3).

STORING EMERGENCY FUEL

Obtain fuel for your alternate heating system and store enough to last several days. Store it in a safe, convenient place such as a garage, carport, or shed away from the house. Do not use your emergency fuel for any other purpose, and check the supply regularly.

COMMUNITY RESOURCES

What resources are available for emergency assistance in your community? There may be town, school, or county plans for coping with emergencies. Your local Red Cross or civil preparedness authorities may have contingency plans and supplies. Find out.

A. Are there stockpiles of fuel available such as coal, oil, or firewood? (Some towns keep emergency supplies of firewood on hand at dumps or highway department sheds. If yours doesn't, perhaps it should.)
B. Are there any emergency supplies of foodstuffs and water? A civil preparedness representative or your County Agent could advise.
C. If your family were forced to leave its home, where could it go? Under what conditions? Schools and municipal buildings often have emergency lighting equipment and heat.
D. You may want to consider a cooperative emergency plan which combines your resources with those of a neighbor.

THE BOAT

Owners might wish to consider purchasing a fireplace and build it into the bulk-head. The purchasing of a prefabricated fireplace which is highly efficient in operation, light in weight easily installed, attractive, and lower in cost than masonry units is recommended. A wood stove is generally a second choice, but be careful that it will not be in the way during a gale. If a prefabricated chimney, fireplace, or stove is purchased, be sure it is Underwriters' Laboratories (UL) and Coast Guard approved.

THE MOBILE HOME

Owners of mobile homes should consider installing a prefabricated sheet metal chimney assembly through a wall or the roof. Mobile homes are particularly well adapted for use of prefabricated chimneys. A properly installed stove will be much more beneficial than a fireplace in a mobile environment. You should also be cautioned that many mobile homes are constructed so tightly that a special means of providing combustion air should be provided or there may not be enough draft or oxygen for complete combustion.

RELATED HEAT LOSS PROBLEMS

Keeping your family warm obviously won't be the only problem you will face if an energy failure strikes your home. Consider the following:

Freezing Pipes

If the heat will be off several hours or more and the temperature well below freezing you will have to protect exposed plumbing. Drain all endangered pipes, including hot water heating pipes in rooms that will not receive emergency heat. Familiarize yourself with your home plumbing and heating layout in advance so you can do the job quickly and thoroughly to avoid repairs later.

It may be necessary to install additional valves to enable you to drain only portions of your system. Don't forget the sink, tub, and shower traps; toilet tanks and bowls; your hot water heater; dish and clothes washers; water pumps; and your furnace boiler, if you have one.

Water for Household Use

If you rely on electricity to run your water pump, a power outage could restrict your water use. Save as much water as possible while draining your system and store it in closed or covered containers, preferably where it will not freeze. In addition to water in pipes, a sizeable amount can be collected from your hot water heater if you have one, and toilet storage tanks. Water from the heating system may be unfit for drinking or other household use.

Lighting

Have a good supply of candles, matches, and at least one kerosene or gas lantern with ample fuel. You should have a dependable flashlight with spare bulbs and batteries. If any of these materials are used when there is no emergency, they should be immediately replenished.

Sanitary Facilities

If your water supply is shut off, sanitation will become a problem. Disconnect the chain or lever attached to the toilet handle to prevent accidental flushes and instruct users to put toilet paper in covered containers. Flush only often enough to prevent clogging. An alternative might be to purchase a portable camper's toilet.

Emergency Cooking

During an emergency, providing hot meals for your family may be a problem. A camp stove can be used or, if necessary, cooking can be done in a fireplace. Keep a supply of meal-in-a-can foods such as stews, soups, canned meats, beans, or spaghetti to supplement dry stores like cereal, bread, dried meats, and cheeses. Freeze dried meals used by campers and backpackers are often excellent foods which can be prepared with a minimum of heat.

Safety

Review all your plans and preparations to ensure the safety of your family. Emergency actions are of little value if they lead to a new or bigger emergency. If you don't already have them, a good fire extinguisher and first aid kit are MUSTS!

REMODELING, BUILDING OR BUYING A HOME

Now would be a particularly appropriate time to think of emergency heating. Consider this feature in shopping for older houses, and include it in construction or renovation plans. Any extra cost of including a "second system" will be more than made up for in peace of mind later.

A. The simplest approach might be to have a capped emergency thimble in a single flue chimney for an emergency stove.

B. More desirable (but costing slightly more) would be to include two or more flues in your new rebuilt chimney to accommodate the furnace AND secondary heating devices such as portable heaters, parlor stoves or Franklin-type fireplaces. The stoves make attractive home features, and a fireplace will add value to the house at least equal to the cost of its construction.

C. A number of modern sheet metal fireplaces, either free-standing or wall mounted, are available which do not require expensive masonry work. They can utilize an easily assembled UL-approved prefabricated chimney pipe which vents through a wall or roof to the outside. One might be attractive in your home. Prefabricated chimneys can also be installed in mobile homes.

D. Depending on the style or design of your house—and its heating system—you might wish to install a second conventional system independent of the first, for emergency heating of a portion of the house. A gas floor or wall furnace large enough to heat one or two rooms would meet emergency heat needs; electric heaters could be good insurance when the gas supply fails.

E. Electric generators should be considered by the rural home-owner, especially if it is part of a farm or business which relies on electricity for operation.

BUYING A WOOD FURNANCE

Wood-burning furnaces come in two basic types. One is the forced-air type that distributes hot air throughout your home by means of ducts. The other is the boiler, for hot water heat.

Building a new home? Either system works well, but forced air has two advantages: add-on humidification and air conditioning. If you are buying a woodburner to replace an existing furnace, buy the kind that matches the present system.

Multi-fuel or wood only? Multi-fuel furnaces can burn both wood and gas or oil. They save you money when you feed them wood. But when you aren't home to stoke, they keep the house warm by burning fossil fuel.

Another way is to achieve the same effect by installing a wood-only furnace in tandem with an existing gas or oil furnace. Set the thermostat on the gas or oil furnace a few degrees lower than the thermostat on the wood burner. Then whenever the wood furnace dies down, the other furnace takes over. For safety, you shouldn't connect the two furnaces to the same chimney flue. An extra chimney for the wood furnace can cost a lot of money. So it might make more sense to sell your existing furnace and buy a multi-fuel unit, which needs just a

single flue. Overall, this will probably be the cheapest way to go, and it will save space in the basement over a two-furnace installation.

What kind of maintenance is needed? Some require a fairly careful cleaning every few weeks. Is the wood fire started automatically, or do you have to kindle it up yourself? How big a log will the furnace take? Longer logs mean less work than shorter ones. And how long will the furnace run on a single loading? Most will go about 12 hours. If you are considering a multi-fuel furnace, what fuel besides wood does the furnace burn? Some manufacturers offer only wood/gas furnaces, some offer wood/oil, and others offer a multi-fuel combination. The best way to compare one furnace against another is to read the owner's manuals and the sales literature.

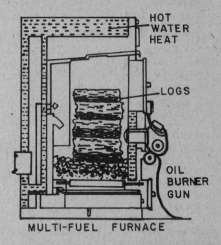

MULTI-FUEL FURNACE

FOR THE UNPREPARED

Your home heat is gone. You've just discovered your system has stopped functioning and may be off for several days. It's cold outside, the temperature is dropping on the inside, and you have a first class emergency on your hands. What can you do?

Your first concern should be to conserve body heat. Keep the people in your household warm while you provide emergency heat. The simplest solution to this problem is to put on suitable clothing, or perhaps get into bed.

Safety is of paramount importance in a heating emergency. Few (if any) Americans have frozen to death in their homes in recent times. Many have perished from burns, smoke inhalation, or carbon monoxide poisoning. Loss of home heat constitutes an emergency, but it needn't result in tragedy.

Handling a heating emergency, once immediate requirements for body heat are met, can be broken down into five steps.

1. Finding a heat source or improvising one.
2. Obtaining fuel.
3. Selecting a room or area to be heated.
4. Setting up, testing, and operating an emergency system.
5. Dealing with related problems caused by heat loss.

Energy Savings Through Automatic Thermostat Controls

There is a myth that says you won't save energy by turning down your thermostat at night because it takes so much energy to warm the building in the morning. But this is untrue. Setting the thermostat back for several hours at a stretch each day during the heating season—up, during the cooling season—will, in a centrally heated and cooled building, save energy. Depending on your geographical location, the amount of energy you can save will range from 9 to 15 percent of what you used before adopting this energy-conserving habit.

Heating Costs Saved with Nighttime Setback

City	Approximate Percentage Saved With 8-Hour Nighttime Setback Of—	
	50° F	10° F
Atlanta, GA	11	15
Boston, MA	7	11
Buffalo, NY	6	10
Chicago, IL	7	11
Cincinnati, OH	8	12
Cleveland, OH	8	12
Columbus, OH	7	11
Dallas, TX	11	15
Denver, CO	7	11
Des Moines, IA	7	11
Detroit, MI	7	11
Kansas City, MO	8	12
Los Angeles, CA	12	16
Louisville, KY	9	13
Madison, WI	5	9
Miami, FL	12	18
Milwaukee, WI	6	10
Minneapolis, MN	5	9
New York, NY	8	12
Omaha, NE	7	11
Philadelphia, PA	8	12
Pittsburgh, PA	7	11
Portland, OR	9	13
Salt Lake City, UT	7	11
San Francisco, CA	10	14
Seattle, WA	8	12
St. Louis, MO	8	12
Syracuse, NY	7	11
Washington, DC	9	13

There are two ways you can accomplish temperature setback and setup: by adjusting the thermostat manually at the proper times or by installing a device that makes the adjustments automatically. The manual technique, of course, requires no special equipment, but it does demand a greater degree of time and attention than many people are willing to put forth day in and day out. An automatic control device, on the other hand, involves some initial investment, but this outlay is more than repaid in dependability and energy savings over a period of time.

How Much Will A Setback Device Save?

The exact energy and cost savings from a setback device are dependent on building design, amount of insulation, climate, temperature setting, and utility rate structures. Several studies have been conducted to estimate the fuel and cost savings that can be realized by using a setback device during both the heating and cooling seasons. The table on the left represents the *approximate* percentage of your heating costs that can be saved in various cities throughout the country for an 8-hour nighttime thermostat setback of 5° F and 10° F.

How To Estimate Cost Savings

From the table, you can estimate what you are likely to save by automatically setting back your thermostat during the heating season from 65° F to either 60° or 55° F at night. For example, if you live in or around Detroit and your heating bills amount to approximately $300 for the heating season, by lowering your thermostat temperature at night from 65° F to 55° F, you could save much as 11 percent of $300, or $33 a heating season. These estimated figures are based on an assumed daytime setting of 65° F.

Types Of Automatic Controls

Two types of automatic controls are now available on the commercial market. One is a device that works with a conventional thermostat. The other type requires replacing the existing thermostat.

Converter Setback Device: This type of control converts any existing thermostat to a timed device. Several variations are available. One is a two-component system in which a temperature control is mounted below the existing thermostat and is connected by wires to a separate timer unit plugged into a wall outlet. If the wires carry low voltage current they can be concealed in the wall, if desired. 110 volt power cords cannot be so concealed. Another is a single-unit device that is attached to the wall below the thermostat and is either plugged into a nearby wall outlet or operated by self-contained batteries.

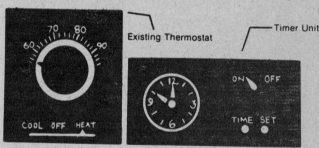

Existing Thermostat — Timer Unit

Replacement Setback Device: This type of control replaces the conventional thermostat entirely and is generally wired to the building's electrical system and heating/cooling system. Several types are available, but this type of device is usually more expensive to buy and costly to install, since it usually requires the additional wiring in existing walls. Its main advantage is that, having all wires hidden, it gives a neater appearance.

Replacement Setback Device

Automatic setback devices are sold in many hardware and department stores as well as building material outlets. In general, converter types sell for less than replacement types and can be installed by a do-it-yourselfer. Most converters retail for less than $40 whereas the initial cost plus the cost of installing a replacement unit may range from $75 to over $100 depending on the model and the type and extent of installation labor required.

IN AN EXTREME EMERGENCY

In an extreme emergency you may have to use a makeshift heating system as illustrated below. Unless a makeshift chimney has been inspected by your local Fire Department and approved by your Insurance Agent you will probably be violating your standard chimney warranty in your Fire Insurance Policy.

SELECTING AN ALTERNATE HEAT SOURCE

What kinds of heating devices do you have which use readily-available fuel such as wood, coal, electricity, gas, or oil? Perhaps you have a space heater you have used in your home, workshop, or shed; perhaps a stove or an electric, gas, or oil heater. Do you have a camp stove? Don't overlook the oven in your gas or electric range. If the fuel is available, turn the range on and open the oven door.

Stoves should be connected to a chimney flue if at all possible. Many older homes have capped stovepipe thimbles in rooms once heated by stoves. Another possibility would be to remove the nonfunctioning furnace pipe from its flue entrance and hook up your stove or heater in its place.

Sometimes a stove pipe can be extended through a window to provide proper venting of gases. NOTE: If no chimney exists, or cannot accomodate a thimble, or the building design prevents your using a prefabricated chimney, a window can be altered to provide proper venting. Replace the glass with a metal sheet through which a temporary stove pipe can be run outside the home. BE SURE NO HEATED SURFACES ARE CLOSE TO THE SASH OR OTHER FLAMMABLE MATERIALS (See figure 4).

1. When setting up emergency stove piping, be careful about running it too close to flammable materials. This is particularly true when using a window-mounted flue. The wood sash is flammable as are curtains or shades that might normally be on the window.
2. Flues and piping for gas-burning appliances are designed primarily to vent vapors and may be unsafe for use with higher temperature oil, coal, or wood smoke.
3. A damper in your emergency flue will help facilitate satisfactory burning and regulation of the heat. Cutting down an excessive draft helps keep the heat in the room and prevents the flue from over-heating. Close the damper as far as possible without reducing combustion or forcing smoke into the room.
4. Natural gas appliances will not burn bottled gas, even in an emergency, without a mechanical conversion. Your local gas supplier has the materials needed for conversion.
5. If you use a catalytic or unvented heater provide plenty of ventilation. Keep a nearby window open at least one inch whenever the device is in use.

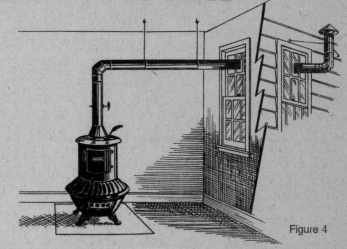

Figure 4

The least desirable solution—but any heat may be better than none—is to rely on a system utilizing a makeshift heater, including campstoves, stackless kerosene space heaters, or industrial-type oil or kerosene jet heaters. *If you must use them, do so only with plenty of ventilation.*

Other possibilities might meet your family's needs depending on the severity of the cold and the resources available around your home. A camping family might have a catalytic heater (a gas or oil-fueled heater which provides heat with no flame.) One of these units can keep one room livable in cold weather. A travel trailer or camper can be inhabited in the winter if it has a heater. More than one farm family has been known to take refuge in the relative warmth of a livestock barn under extreme conditions. For shorter periods, there is the family car, a last resort which will be dangerous without proper ventilation.

Bed may be the safest, warmest place for short periods. Use of adequate blankets and coverings will trap and conserve vital body heat, and two or more people in the same bed can share heat. This is an especially good way to keep children warm.

Don't overlook the possibility of solar heat. An appreciable amount of heat can be gained through large windows on the southern side of the house. Sunlight can give a good boost to morale, too!

The Boston Globe Thursday, December 22, 1977

Wood-burning stoves alarm fire officials

There are no state standards for the quality of manufacture of wood stoves sold in Massachusetts. The Building Code Commission this month ordered a six-month moratorium on such regulations while minimum standards are being drafted.

And James Cosgrove of the state Public Safety D... ...mit-

Faulty Wood Stoves Blamed in House Fires

...allatio.
...official.

Spurred by increasing reports of serious fires attributed to faulty wood stoves, local and state building inspectors are beginning to tighten controls.

...spreading problem of house fires

...ove and selling it.

There are no figures on the number of house fires touched off by faulty wood stoves, he said, but "from reports coming back to us, there are quite a few."

PROVIDING FUEL FOR HEATING

Many combustibles can be considered for fuel. Some of the common ones include:

Furnace coal	Alcohol	Firewood and scraps
Cannel coal	Newspapers, magazines	Motor oil
Furnace oil	Charcoal fluid lighter	Fats, grease
Wood chips	Kerosene, gasoline	Corncobs
Campstove fuel	Stove Coal	Charcoal briquets

1. Coal can be burned in a fireplace or stove if a grate is fashioned to hold it, allowing air to circulate underneath.

   "Hardware cloth" screening placed on a standard wood grate will keep coal from falling through.

2. Paper "logs" can be made by rolling newspapers or magazines tightly into small log-sized bundles, which can be burned if they are stacked to allow proper air circulation.

3. There may be plenty of burnable wood around, including lumber and furniture if the situation is critical.

   Store fuels you will be using in a handy place, but not in the heated area. This is particularly true for highly combustible items such as gasoline, kerosene, and papers.

WHICH ROOM SHOULD BE HEATED?

The decision may be dictated by location of a fireplace, stove, or chimney flue. Be guided by the following:
1. Confine emergency heat to a small area.
2. Try to select a room on the "warm" side of the house away from prevailing cold winds. Avoid rooms with large windows or uninsulated walls. Interior bathrooms probably have the lowest air leakage and heat loss. Your basement may be a good place in cold weather because of the heat gain from the earth.
3. Isolate the room from the rest of the house by keeping doors closed, hanging bedding or heavy drapes over entryways or erecting temporary partitions of cardboard or plywood.
4. Hang drapes, bedding, shower curtains, etc., over doors and windows, especially at night.

CHECK YOUR EFFORTS FOR SAFETY

As soon as emergency heating is working and the room protected against exterior cold, stop and appraise the safety of your situation. If there is any hazard or question of safety posed by the emergency heating, make changes immediately. Check carefully for fire hazards.

All heaters except electric heaters should be vented to provide oxygen for complete combustion and to safely remove exhaust gases and smoke.

DO NOT ATTEMPT TO BURN ANYTHING LARGER THEN CANDLES IN YOUR HOME WITHOUT PROVIDING ADEQUATE VENTILATION TO THE OUTSIDE.

Asphyxiation from lack of oxygen or poisonous gases is a great danger when there is not enough ventilation. There is no simple rule for determining how much ventilation you need. For safety, provide cross ventilation by opening a window an inch on each side of a room. It is better to let in some cold air than to take a chance of not having enough air.

As an additional safety factor you should have a firewatch whenever emergency heat is being used. One person should stay awake to watch for fire and to detect the possibility of inadequate ventilation. Drowsiness is one sign of carbon monoxide poisoning. If the firewatch feels sleepy, it may be a sign of not enough ventilation.

If you have not already done so, set up some firefighting items near your emergency heating device. Dry powder fire extinguishers will put out most types of burning materials. Sand, salt, baking soda, or water can be used on most non oil materials. A tarpaulin, or heavy blanket, can be used for smothering flames. Post your local fire department's telephone number conspicuously near your telephone. Finally, discuss safety, firefighting techniques, and a home evacuation plan with all members of your family. Be prepared for the worst.

PART 9: SOLAR HOT WATER SYSTEMS
Functional Description

The basic function of a solar domestic hot water system is the collection and conversion of solar radiation into usable energy. This is accomplished—in general terms—in the following manner: Solar radiation is absorbed by a *collector*, placed in *storage* as required, with or without the use of a *transport* medium, and *distributed* to point of use. The performance of each operation is maintained by automatic or manual *controls*. An *auxiliary energy system* is usually available both to supplement the output provided by the solar system and to provide for the total energy demand should the solar system become inoperable.

The parts of a solar system—collector, storage, distribution, transport, controls and auxiliary energy—may vary widely in design, operation, and performance. They may be arranged in numerous combinations dependent on function, component compatibility, climatic conditions, required performance, site characteristics, and architectural requirements.

Of the numerous concepts presently being developed for the collection of solar radiation, the relatively simple flat-plate *collector* has the widest application. It consists of an absorber plate, usually made of metal and coated black to increase absorption of the sun's energy. The plate is insulated on its underside and covered with one or more transparent cover plates to trap heat within the collector and reduce convective losses from the absorber plate. The captured heat is removed from the absorber plate by means of a heat transfer fluid, generally air or water. The fluid is heated as it passes through or near the absorber plate and then transported to points of use, or to storage, depending on energy demand. (Most solar hot water systems use liquid heat transfer fluids.)

The *storage* of thermal energy is the second item of importance since there will be an energy demand during the evening, or on sunless days when solar collection cannot occur. Heat is stored when the energy delivered by the sun and captured by the collector exceeds the demand at the point of use. In some cases, it is necessary to transfer heat from the collector to storage by means of a heat exchanger. In other cases, transfer is made by direct contact of the heat transfer fluid with the storage medium.

The *distribution* component receives heat energy from the collector or storage, and dispenses it at points of use as hot water.

The *controls* of a solar system perform the sensing, evaluation and response functions required to operate the system in the desired mode. For example, when the collector temperature is sufficiently higher than storage temperature, the controls will cause the heat transfer fluid in storage to circulate through the collector and accumulate solar heat.

An *auxiliary energy* system provides the supply of energy when stored energy is depleted due to severe weather or clouds. The auxiliary system, using conventional fuels such as oil, gas, electricity, or wood provides the required heat until solar energy is available again.

Most solar systems can be characterized as either active or passive in their operation.

An *active solar system* is generally classified as one in which an energy resource—in addition to solar—is used for the transfer of thermal energy. This additional energy, generated on or off the site, is required for pumps or other heat transfer medium moving devices for system operation. Generally, the collection, storage, and distribution of thermal energy is achieved by moving a transfer medium throughout the system with the assistance of pumping power.

A *passive solar system*, on the other hand, is generally classified as one where solar energy alone is used for the transfer of thermal energy. Energy other than solar is not required for pumps or other heat transfer medium moving devices for system operation. Collection, storage, and distribution is achieved by natural heat transfer phenomena employing convection, radiation and conduction.

**A Residence with Solar Collectors
Incorporated Into the Roof.**

Operational Description

The solar hot water system usually is designed to preheat water from the incoming water supply prior to passage through a conventional water heater. The domestic hot water preheat system can be combined with a solar heating system or designed as a separate system. Both situations are illustrated below.

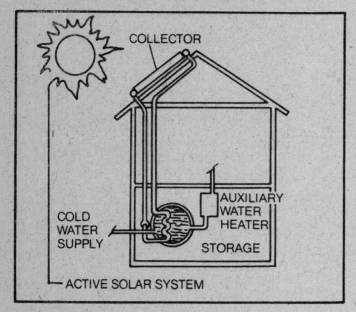

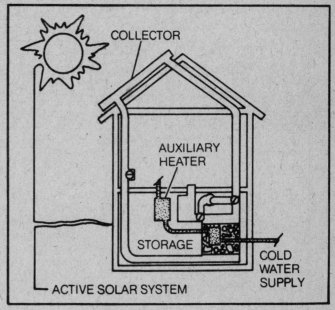

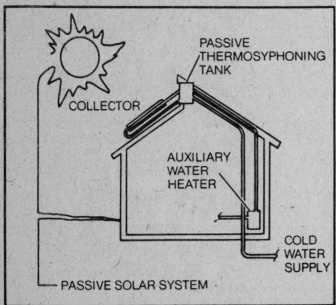

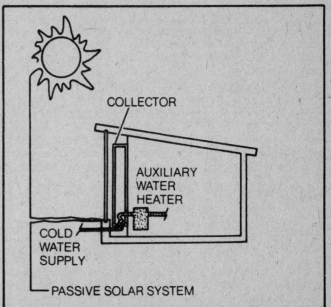

Domestic Hot Water Preheating—Separate System. Domestic hot water preheating may be the only solar system included in many designs. An active solar system is shown in the upper figure and a passive thermosyphoning arrangement in the lower.

Domestic Hot Water Preheating—Combined System. Domestic hot water is preheated as it passes through heat storage enroute to the conventional water heater. An active solar system using air for heat transport is shown in the upper figure and a passive solar system in the lower.

Basics of Solar Energy Utilization

Collector Orientation and Tilt

Solar collectors must be oriented and tilted within prescribed limits to receive the optimum level of solar radiation for system operation and performance.

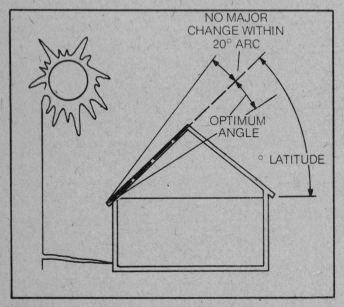

Collector Tilt for Domestic Hot Water. The optimum collector tilt for domestic water heating alone is usually equal to the site latitude. Tilt angle for solar hot water can be latitude ± 15 degrees for optimum performance; a 15 degree variation does not cause a major impact.

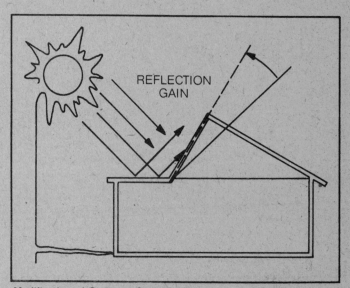

Modification of Optimum Collector Tilt. A greater gain in solar radiation collection sometimes may be achieved by tilting the collector away from the optimum in order to capture radiation reflected from adjacent ground or building surfaces. The corresponding reduction of radiation directly striking the collector, due to non-optimum tilt, should be recognized when considering this option.

Snowfall Consideration. The snowfall characteristics of an area may influence the appropriateness of these optimum collector tilts. Snow buildup on the collector, or drifting in front of the collector, should be avoided.

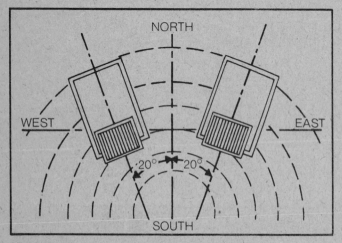

Collector Orientation. A collector orientation of 20 degrees to either side of true South is acceptable. However, local climate and collector type may influence the choice between East or West deviations.

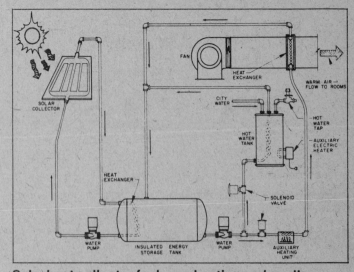

Solar heat collector for home heating and cooling

Shading of Collector

Another issue related to both collector orientation and tilt is shading. Solar collectors should be located on the building or site so that unwanted shading of the collectors by adjacent structures, landscaping or building elements does not occur. In addition, considerations for avoiding shading of the collector by other collectors should also be made. Collector shading by elements surrounding the site must also be addressed.

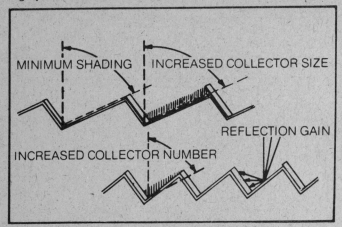

Self-Shading of Collector. Avoiding all self-shading for a bank of parallel collectors during useful collection hours (9 AM and 3 PM) results in designing for the lowest angle of incidence with large spaces between collectors. It may be desirable therefore to allow some self-shading at the end of solar collection hours, in order to increase collector size or to design a closer spacing of collectors, thus increasing solar collection area.

Shading of Collector by Building Elements. Chimneys, parapets, fire walls, dormers, and other building elements can cast shadows on adjacent roof-mounted solar collectors, as well as on vertical wall collectors. The drawing to the right shows a house with a 45° south-facing collector at latitude 40° North. By mid-afternoon portions of the collector are shaded by the chimney, dormer, and the offset between the collector on the garage. Careful attention to the placement of building elements and to floor plan arrangement is required to assure that unwanted collector shading does not occur.

Active Systems

Active solar systems are characterized by collectors, thermal storage units and transfer media, in an assembly which requires additional mechanical energy to convert and transfer the solar energy into thermal energy. The following discussion of active solar systems serves as an introduction to a range of active concepts which have been constructed.

Domestic hot water can be preheated either by circulating the potable water supply itself through the collector, or by passing the supply line through storage enroute to a conventional water heater. Three storage-related preheat systems are shown below.

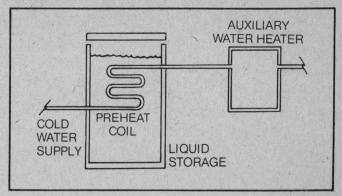

Preheat Coil in Storage. Water is passed through a suitably sized coil placed in storage enroute to the conventional water heater. Unless the preheat coil has a protective double-wall construction, this method can only be used for solar systems employing non-toxic storage media.

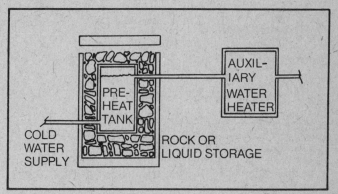

Preheat Tank in Storage. In this system, the domestic hot water preheat tank is located within the heat storage. The water supply passes through storage to the preheat tank where it is heated and stored, and later piped to a conventional water heater as needed. A protective double-wall construction again will be necessary unless a non-toxic storage medium is used.

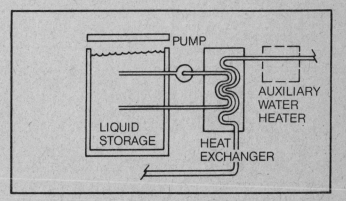

Preheat Outside of Storage. In this preheat method, the heat transfer liquid in storage is pumped through a separate heat exchanger to be used for domestic hot water preheating. This separate heat exchanger could be the conventional water heater itself. However, if the liquid from storage is toxic, the required separation of liquids is achieved by the use of a double-wall exchanger, as diagrammed, in which the water supply simply passes through enroute to the conventional water heater.

Collector Mounting

Flat-plate collectors are generally mounted on the ground or on a building in a fixed position at prescribed angles of solar exposure—angles which vary according to the geographic location, collector type, and the use of the absorbed heat. Flat-plate collectors may be mounted in four general ways as illustrated below.

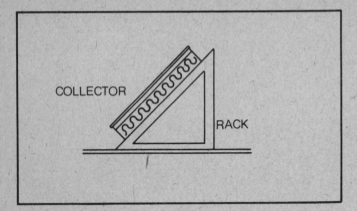

Rack Mounting. Collectors can be mounted at the prescribed angle on a structural frame located on the ground or attached to the building. The structural connection between the collector and the frame and the frame and the building or site must be adequate to resist any impact loads such as wind.

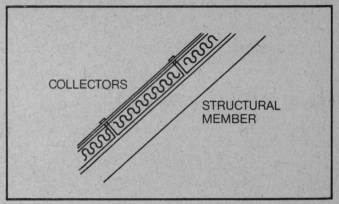

Direct Mounting. Collectors can be mounted directly on the roof surface. Generally, the collectors are placed on a water-proof membrane on top of the roof sheathing. The finished roof surface, together with the necessary collector structural attachments and flashing, are then built up around the collector. A weatherproof seal between the collector and the roof must be maintained, or leakage, mildew, and rotting may occur.

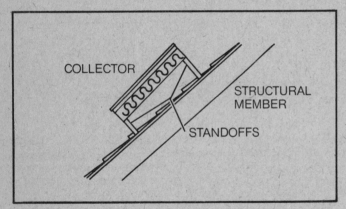

Stand-Off Mounting. Elements that separate the collector from the finished roof surface are known as stand-offs. They allow air and rain water to pass under the collector thus minimizing problems of mildew and leakage. The stand-offs must also have adequate structural properties. Stand-offs are often used to support collectors at an angle other than that of the roof to optimize collector tilt.

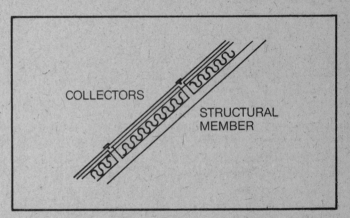

Integral Mounting. Unlike the previous three component collectors which can be applied or mounted separately, integral mounting places the collector within the roof construction itself. Thus, the collector is attached to and supported by the structural framing members. In addition, the top of the collector serves as the finished roof surface. Weather tightness is again crucial to avoid problems of water damage and mildew. This method of mounting is frequently used for site built collectors.

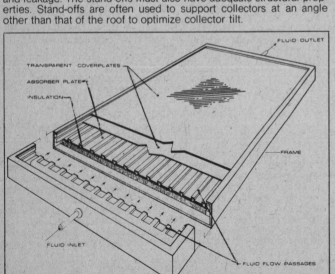

Detailed view of a typical solar collector.

Component Description

As noted in the functional description, a solar domestic hot water system is composed of numerous individual parts and pieces including: collectors; storage; a distribution network with pipes, pumps and valves; insulation; a system of manual or automatic controls; and possibly heat exchangers, expansion tanks and filters. These parts are assembled in a variety of combinations depending on function, component compatibility, climatic conditions, required performance, site characteristics and architectural requirements, to form a solar domestic hot water system. Some components that are unique to the collector system or that are used in an unconventional manner are briefly illustrated and discussed in the next few pages.

Flat-Plate Collectors

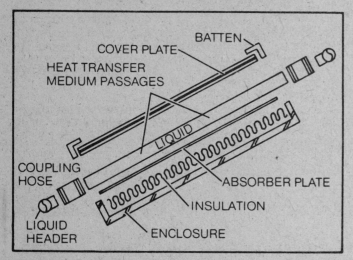

The flat-plate collector is a common solar collection device used for domestic water heating. Most collectors are designed to use liquid (usually treated water) as the heat transfer medium. However, air systems are available for domestic water heating. Most flat-plate collectors consist of the same general components, as illustrated below.

Batten. Battens serve to hold down the cover plate(s) and provide a weather tight seal between the enclosure and the cover.

Cover Plate. The cover plate usually consists of one or more layers of glass or plastic film or combinations thereof. The cover plate is separated from the absorber plate to reduce reradiation and to create an air space, which traps heat by reducing convective losses. This space between the cover and absorber can be evacuated to further reduce convective losses.

Heat Transfer Fluid Passage. Tubes are attached above, below or integral with an absorber plate for the purpose of transferring thermal energy from the absorber plate to a heat transfer medium. The largest variation in flat-plate collector design occurs with this component and its combination with the absorber plate. Tube on plate, integral tube and sheet, open channel flow, corrugated sheets, deformed sheets, extruded sheets and finned tubes are some of the techniques used.

Absorber Plate. Since the absorber plate must have a good thermal bond with the fluid passages, an absorber plate integral with the heat transfer media passages is common. The absorber plate is usually metallic, and normally treated with a surface coating which improves absorptivity. Black or dark paints or selective coatings are used for this purpose. The design of this passage and plate combination helps determine a solar system's effectiveness.

Insulation. Insulation is employed to reduce heat loss through the back of the collector. The insulation must be suitable for the high temperature that may occur under no-flow or dry-plate conditions, or even normal collection operation. Thermal decomposition and outgassing of the insulation must be prevented.

Enclosure. The enclosure is a container for all the above components. The assembly is usually weatherproof. Preventing dust, wind and water from coming in contact with the cover plate and insulation is essential to maintaining collector performance.

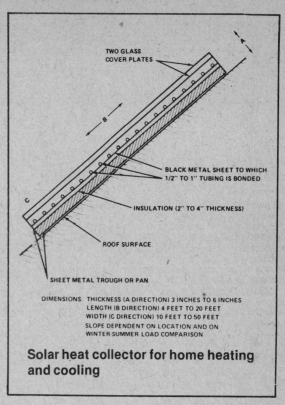

Solar heat collector for home heating and cooling

Heat Exchangers

A heat exchanger is a device for transferring thermal energy from one fluid to another. In some solar systems, a heat exchanger may be required between the transfer medium circulated through the collector and the storage medium or between the storage and the distribution medium. Three types of heat exchangers that are most commonly used for these purposes are illustrated below.

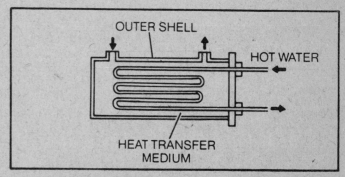

Shell and Tube. This type of heat exchanger is used to transfer heat from a circulating transfer medium to another medium used in storage or in distribution. Shell and tube heat exchangers consist of an outer casing or shell surrounding a bundle of tubes. The water to be heated is normally circulated in the tubes and the hot liquid is circulated in the shell. Tubes are usually metal such as steel, copper or stainless steel. A single shell and tube heat exchanger *cannot be used* for heat transfer from a toxic liquid to potable water because double separation is not provided and the toxic liquid may enter the potable water supply, in a case of tube failure.

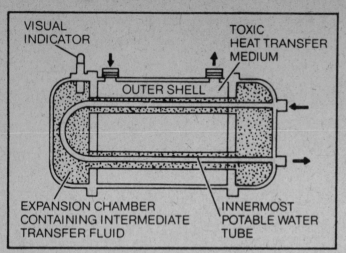

VISUAL INDICATOR

TOXIC HEAT TRANSFER MEDIUM

OUTER SHELL

EXPANSION CHAMBER CONTAINING INTERMEDIATE TRANSFER FLUID

INNERMOST POTABLE WATER TUBE

Shell and Double Tube. This type of heat exchanger is similar to the previous one except that a secondary chamber is located within the shell to surround the potable water tube. The heated toxic liquid then circulates inside the shell but around this second tube. An intermediary non-toxic heat transfer liquid is then located between the two tube circuits. As the toxic heat transfer medium circulates through the shell, the intermediary liquid is heated, which in turn heats the potable water supply circulating through the innermost tube. This heat exchanger can be equipped with a sight glass to detect leaks by a change in color—toxic liquid often contains a dye—or by a change in the liquid level in the intermediary chamber, which would indicate a failure in either the outer shell or intermediary tube lining.

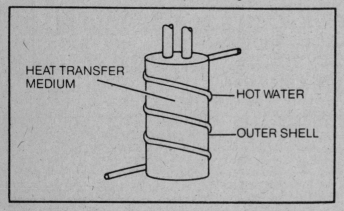

HEAT TRANSFER MEDIUM

HOT WATER

OUTER SHELL

Double Wall. Another method of providing a double separation between the transfer medium and the potable water supply consists of tubing or a plate coil wrapped around and bonded to a tank. The potable water is heated as it circulates through the coil or through the tank. When this method is used, the tubing coil must be adequately insulated to reduce heat losses.

Evaluating Solar Hot Water Systems

A typical solar domestic hot water system for an average family of four may cost $2,200 uninstalled, depending on geographic location, collector efficiency and other factors. Installation costs vary greatly on a case by case basis depending on the design of the home and on any structural modifications required. The system should be HUD Program approved; contact your State Energy Office.

Two important factors are first cost and collector efficiency. Both factors must be considered when comparing collectors. Thus a relatively inexpensive collector with a low efficiency may be a poor choice when compared to a more expensive one that captures and delivers the sun's energy more efficiently. All other things being equal, the collector that delivers more *heat per dollar* should be selected.

Durability. How long is it expected to last? Is it weatherproof and does it shed water?

Ease of Repair. If something goes wrong, who will fix it, how long will it take to fix it, and are repair parts easily obtainable? And what will various repairs cost?

Susceptibility to Either Freezing or Overheating. There are a number of adequate solutions to both problems, and the collector must have protection for both extremes built in. In addition, if antifreeze fluid is used in the collector, it must not mix with water for domestic use.

Protection Against Corrosion. Metal corrosion can cause irreparable damage to a solar system and shorten a system's life span. More importantly, corrosion can cause serious health problems if the water is used directly by the user. The three metals commonly used in collectors are copper, steel and aluminum. Inhibitors are usually added to prevent corrosion in most systems. Copper will function over a long period without inhibitors, while steel and aluminum may fail quickly without special protection. With inhibited water, all three will last indefinitely as long as inhibition is maintained.

Protection Against Leaks. The greater the number of joints, the greater the possibility of leakage. Some liquid collectors using channel systems have reduced the need for soldered joints considerably without affecting efficiency. Know what happens if a leak occurs, how it will be fixed, who will fix it and how much it will cost.

Consumer Protection. Try to obtain the names of other buyers, and learn whether the buyer is satisfied with its performance and whether the collector has lived up to the claims of the seller.

Insulation. The pipes, ducts, and back parts of collectors, and storage tank should be insulated to prevent heat loss. This is true of inside and outside pipes and ducts. Avoid use of heating tapes to prevent freezing. They may use more energy than the solar system saves.

Pitch of Pipes. The flow of water in pipes has to be positive. If the collector is the drain down type, there cannot be any traps in the external pipes where water can collect and possibly freeze. Pipes and collectors need to be pitched to achieve drain down.

Bleeding mechanism. Air has a habit of getting into systems even though they are watertight. Facility should be provided for bleeding the system. An expansion tank, or room in storage for expansion, should also be included.

Fans and Pumps. These items use electricity and hence should not be any bigger than necessary to perform. If they are too big then they will reduce the total energy savings. A time elapsed meter can be installed to see if the fans or pumps are running for too long a period. Sometimes they can be on when not needed but since they are quiet the homeowner is not aware that they are on. Pumps should be located below tank water level.

Tests. The system should be taken through a complete operating test before acceptance by the owner. All controls should be confirmed as working and all leaks should be fixed. There should be confirmation that the collector does increase the temperature in storage. If the system is a drain-down type there should be evidence that the system will drain-down properly.

Controls and Valves. These items should be corrosive resistant and as silent as possible. In a system that connects directly to the potable water supply inhibitors or anti-freeze cannot be used. In this case the controls and valves should be brass.

PART 10: NATIONAL ENERGY ACT OF 1978 YOUR ENERGY TAX CREDITS

Residential Conservation

Taxpayers can receive tax credits for installing energy-saving materials in their homes amounting to 15 percent of the first $2,000 spent on qualifying equipment, up to a maximum of $300. The credit can be subtracted from taxes due.

The credit could be applied to any equipment installed after April 20, 1977, the day President Carter announced his energy plan. The credit would be for existing dwellings only (in existence as of the effective date of the act). The credit would be effective through Dec. 31, 1985. The installation must be made in the taxpayer's principal residence. Eligible for the credit are owners, renters, and owners of cooperatives or condominiums.

A taxpayer who qualified for a tax credit in excess of the tax he owes could carry the credit forward on future tax returns through the taxable years ending Jan. 1, 1988. However, for expenditures made in 1977, a credit could only be claimed on the taxpayer's 1978 tax return. No refunds for credit in excess of taxes due would be allowed.

Eligible for the credit would be insulation, furnace replacement burners, devices for modifying flue openings, electrical or mechanical furnace ignition systems that replace a gas pilot light, storm or thermal doors or windows, clock thermostats, caulking or weatherstripping and other items specified by the Treasury Department as increasing energy efficiency in the dwelling. Items include automatic energy-saving thermostats and meters that display the cost of energy usage.

Residential, Solar Wind

A taxpayer could receive up to 30 percent of the first $2,000 spent and 20 percent on the next $8,000 spent on qualifying equipment. The maximum credit would be $2,200. Like the residential credit, it would be available for equipment installed from April 20, 1977, to Dec. 31, 1985, and taxpayers could carry forward any excess credit, except on 1977 expenditures. No refunds would be allowed. Unlike the conservation credit, this credit would apply to both new and existing homes.

Eligible equipment includes solar space and hot water heating, wind energy equipment, geothermal equipment and other "renewable energy" equipment, including "passive solar" energy installations. Passive solar energy relies on the design of the building and the use of thermal storage mass such as masonry walls. In a typical passive system, sunshine enters the structure through a south-facing window, is stored as heat in a stone wall and is radiated back during the night. The Congress adopted language to eliminate from eligibility anything that serves a "significant" structural function, such as extra thick walls. Solar electricity devices, such as photovoltaic cells, leased solar energy equipment and wind transportation equipment would not qualify.

Energy Conservation Measures

A variety of tempting incentives are available to middle-class homeowners and low-income renters for installing such fuel-saving measures as insulation and solar heating equipment. Electric and gas utilities would play a major role in informing ratepayers about their individual energy conservation needs.

Utility Conservation Program

Under the National Energy Act, large gas and electric utilities are required to inform their residential customers about ways to save energy, suggesting the installation of appropriate equipment, and estimating possible energy savings from such improvements. They also must provide lists of businesses in the area that will finance, supply, and install the energy-conserving measures suggested under the bill. Also, utilities would have to offer to inspect each customer's home to advise him on his individual need for equipment or energy-saving practices to plug energy leaks. Utilities could act as a "project manager," or contractor, by offering to arrange for the installation and financing of residential conservation measures by other businesses and lending institutions. The customer could repay a lending institution for an energy conservation loan through payments on his regular utility bill.

Small Utility Loans

Utilities could make small loans of no more than $300 for the purchase or installation of specified conservation measures. The Department of Energy can expand this list or make modifications to reflect the varying climatic needs of different regions.

The conservation measures specified in the conference report include caulking and weatherstripping of doors and windows; new, efficient furnaces or boilers to replace old inefficient ones; ceiling, attic, wall and floor insulation; water heater insulation; storm windows and doors; special heat-absorbing or heat-reflective glazed windows; and solar wind-power equipment, including water heating, space heating, and cooling.

Three Devices Eligible For Higher Loans

If a residential customer is purchasing and installing one or more of the three special devices, a utility may make a loan for more than $300, if the cost of these measures is greater than $300. The three special types of equipment are (1) clock thermostats; (2) devices to increase the efficiency of furnaces, such as flue constrictors that limit the amount of heat escaping up the chimney, and electrical or mechanical furnace ignition systems that replace standing gas pilot lights; and (3) load management devices, primarily meters that measure how much energy has been used at different times of the day so that the utility can charge a reduced rate for off-peak power use.

Furnace retrofit devices alone could save the consumer 26 percent of his gas bill and 30 percent of his oil heating bill; these devices could save a significant amount of energy at a small expense. The utility can charge a reduced rate for off-peak power use. Utilities are prohibited from installing any conservation measures, except for the above three special devices. The utility program is directed at owners of single-family homes or very small apartment buildings (four units or less).

Solar Home Loans

Homeowners at all income levels could receive loans at reasonable interest rates for solar heating, cooling, and hot water equipment purchased and installed after the date of enactment. Banks and other community lenders could make solar loans of up to $8,000 each at interest rates ranging from about 7 percent to 12 percent for periods of up to 15 years. Buildings with up to four family dwelling units would be eligible. Another provision of importance to home buyers would increase by up to 20 percent the limits on federally-insured loans; this provision would apply to the loan programs of the Federal Housing Administration and the Farmers Home Administration. For example, an individual interested in buying a solar home with a low-interest FHA loan could exceed the current FHA mortgage limit of $60,000 to buy a solar home valued at $72,000.

The definition of energy-conserving improvements eligible for federal home improvement loan insurance is expanded to include wind energy equipment and active or "passive" solar energy equipment. Passive solar uses building design to make maximum use of solar energy through such means as south-facing windows.

Energy Credits for Individuals

Introduction

Congress has provided tax incentives to encourage energy conservation and the development of alternate energy sources. This publication explains the new tax credits that may be claimed by individuals who installed energy-saving components or solar, geothermal, or wind-powered equipment in their homes after April 19, 1977. For solar, geothermal, or wind-powered equipment, the credit is also available for installations in connection with construction or reconstruction of dwellings before April 20, 1977, provided the original occupancy by the taxpayers began after April 19, 1977.

You claim the credits on line 45 of your Form 1040 for 1978. The amount of credit is computed on Form 5695, which you attach to your return. All eligible expenditures from April 20, 1977, through the end of 1978 are included in computing your credit for 1978. For this purpose, expenditures are generally treated as made when the original installation is completed. You may not amend a 1977 return to claim an energy credit for that year. You may not claim an energy credit on Form 1040A.

Fiscal year return. If you file your return on a fiscal year basis, you may not take the credit until your first tax year beginning after 1977. Your eligible expenditures, however, from April 20, 1977, through the end of your fiscal year may be combined in determining your energy credit for the first tax year.

Two distinct energy credits make up the residential energy credit, each with its own conditions and limitations. These credits are based on:

1) Expenditures for home energy conservation; and
2) Expenditures for renewable energy source property.

Residential Energy Credit

The residential energy credit is made up of the *credit for energy conservation expenditures* (15% of the first $2,000 spent on components to conserve energy, or a maximum credit of $300) plus the *credit for renewable energy source expenditures* (30% of the first $2,000 plus 20% of the next $8,000 spent on solar, geothermal, or wind-powered equipment, or a maximum credit of $2,200).

The credit is based on the cost of items installed after April 19, 1977, and before January 1, 1986, regardless of when the items were actually purchased. However, solar, geothermal, or wind-powered items that were installed in a newly constructed or reconstructed residence before April 20, 1977, will qualify for the credit if the residence was first occupied by the taxpayer after April 19, 1977. The cost of qualifying items includes the cost of their original installation.

Your residential energy credit must amount to at least $10 in any one year before it may be claimed. This $10 minimum applies *before* you consider the limitation to tax described in the following paragraph. The minimum applies to either joint or separate returns.

The credit may not exceed the amount of tax for which you are otherwise liable. Specifically, it is limited to the tax on line 37, Form 1040, minus the credits on lines 38 through 44, Form 1040.

Carryover of unused credit. You may carry over an unused credit (that you may not use because it exceeds your tax liability) to the next tax year. An unused credit may continue to be carried over to later tax years through 1987. (For a fiscal year filer, an unused credit may be carried over through the fiscal year beginning in 1987.)

You must reduce the basis of your residence by the amount of residential energy credit allowed, if the items for which the credit is taken are properly added to the basis of the residence.

Both owners and renters of dwellings are eligible for the credit, provided they actually pay for the qualifying items.

Stockholders of cooperative housing corporations and owners of condominium units may claim a credit based on their allocable share of qualifying expenditures made by the cooperative housing corporation or condominium management association for the benefit of the common owners. For a stockholder of a cooperative housing corporation, the allocable share of the cooperative's expenditures is proportionate to the stockholder's share of the cooperative's total outstanding stock.

If you own or rent your residence jointly with others, the overall limits on qualifying expenditures apply to the combined expenditures of all the owners or renters. If the actual amount spent is greater than the limits, the maximum credit must be apportioned to the joint owners or renters based on the portion of the total expenditures that each contributed. The fact that one joint occupant may be unable to claim all or part of the credit, either because of insufficient tax liability or because of not meeting the $10 minimum credit, has no effect on the computation of the credit for the other joint occupants.

Business use of home. If more than 20% of the use of an energy-conserving or renewable energy source item is for business purposes, you must allocate the expenditure for the item between the business use and the residential use. Only the expenditure allocable to the residential use qualifies for the credit. A swimming pool is not considered used for residential purposes.

Home Energy Conservation Expenditures

You are entitled to a credit of 15% of the first $2,000 you spend on components to conserve energy in your home. You are eligible for the credit when the original installation of the components is completed. The full $2,000 of energy-saving items need not be installed in a single tax year. However, if the qualifying items are installed over a period of more than one tax year, the 15% credit must be claimed for the tax years in which the items are installed, except that expenditures for items installed from April 20, 1977, through the end of 1978 must be combined in computing the 1978 credit. A new $2,000 limit applies to each subsequent principal residence in which you live.

Example 1. In September 1977 you purchase and install $500 of insulation. In February 1978 you install storm windows costing $1,500. If you file your tax returns on a calendar year basis, you may claim a $300 (15% of $2,000) credit on your 1978 return. You may not amend your 1977 return to claim a credit for that year.

Example 2. The facts are the same as in Example 1, but you move to another home in 1979 and spend additional amounts for energy-saving components for the new home. You are eligible for another credit of up to $300 for these expenditures, provided the other conditions are met. You may claim the credit for your additional energy-saving expenditures on the new home, even though the previous owner of your new home had claimed a credit for energy-saving expenditures on it.

Principal residence. The dwelling on which you install the qualified energy-saving components must be your principal residence, must be located in the United States, and must have been substantially completed before April 20, 1977. To qualify for the credit, a dwelling is considered your principal residence beginning 30 days before the date you occupy it.

The energy-saving components you install must be new, must be expected to last at least 3 years, and must meet performance and quality standards to be specified by the Secretary of the Treasury. As of the date of this publication, no performance and quality standards

have been issued. However, components purchased before the performance and quality standards are published need not meet these standards.

Qualifying energy-saving components include the following:

Insulation designed to reduce heat loss or heat gain of a residence or water heater

Storm or thermal windows or doors for the exterior of the dwelling

Caulking or weather stripping of exterior doors or windows

Clock thermostats or other automatic energy-saving setback thermostats

Furnace modifications designed to increase fuel efficiency, including replacement burners, modified flue openings, and ignition systems that replace a gas pilot light

Meters that display the cost of energy usage

Additional items, when specified by the Secretary of the Treasury as increasing the energy efficiency of the dwelling. As of the date of this publication, no additional items have been so specified.

Insulation is any item that is specifically and primarily designed to reduce heat loss or gain of a dwelling or water heater. It includes, but is not limited to, materials made of fiberglass, rock wool, cellulose, styrofoam, urea-based foam, urethane, vermiculite, perlite, polystyrene, reflective insulation, and extruded polystyrene foam. It is installed in one of the following applications:

Ceiling insulation, which is installed on the surface of the ceiling facing the building interior or between the heated top living level and the unheated attic space;

Wall insulation, which is installed on the surface or in the cavity of an exterior wall;

Floor insulation, which is installed between the first level heated space of the dwelling and the unheated space beneath it, including a basement or crawl space;

Insulation for hot bare pipes, which is installed around the exterior of the pipes;

Roof insulation, which is placed on the surface of the roof facing the building interior or between a roof deck and its water repellent roof surface;

Exterior insulation for a hot water heater, which is placed around the exterior of the tank; and

Insulation for forced air ducts, which is wrapped around the exterior of the ducts.

Insulation does not include items that are primarily structural or decorative. For example, carpets, drapes, wood paneling, and exterior siding do not qualify although they may have been designed in part to have an insulating effect.

Storm or thermal windows include the following:

1) A window placed outside or inside an ordinary or prime window, creating an air space and providing greater resistance to heat flow and reduced air infiltration.

2) A window with enhanced resistance to heat flow through the glass area by multi-glazing, or with reduced air infiltration through weather stripping. Multi-glazing is an arrangement in which two or more sheets of glazing material are fixed in a window frame to create one or more closed insulating spaces.

3) A window in which the glazed area consists of glass or other glazing materials with heat-absorbing or heat-reflecting properties that reduce the penetration of radiant heat through the window.

Storm or thermal doors include the following:

1) A second door, installed exterior to an existing outer door, to provide greater resistance to heat flow and to reduce air infiltration.

2) A prime exterior door with enhanced resistance to heat flow through the door area because of reduced air infiltration through weather stripping and reduced heat flow through insulating wood or plastic frame material or metal material incorporating thermal breaks.

3) A glass door in which the glazed area is multi-glazed, or consists of glass or other materials with heat-absorbing or heat-reflecting properties that reduce the penetration of radiant heat through the door.

Caulking consists of non-rigid materials placed in the joints of buildings to reduce the passage of air and moisture.

Weather stripping consists of narrow strips of flexible material placed over or in moveable joints of windows and doors to reduce the passage of air and moisture.

Automatic energy-saving setback thermostats are devices designed to reduce energy consumption by regulating the demand on the heating or cooling systems in which they are installed. These thermostats use a temperature control device for interior spaces incorporating more than one temperature control point, and a clock or other mechanism for switching from one control point to another.

Furnace replacement burners are devices for gas or oil-fired heating equipment that:

1) Mix the fuel with air and ignite the fuel-air mixture,

2) Are an integral part of a gas or oil-fired furnace or boiler, including the combustion chamber,

3) Replace an existing furnace burner, and

4) Are designed to achieve a reduction in the amount of fuel consumed as a result of increased combustion efficiency.

Flue opening modifications are dampers that, when installed in the pipe connecting the furnace to the chimney, conserve energy by substantially stopping the flow of air to the chimney when the furnace is not in operation.

Furnace ignition systems are electrical or mechanical devices that, when installed in a gas-fired heating system, ignite the fuel and replace a gas pilot light.

Items that do not qualify for the credit include heat pumps, fluorescent lights, wood- or peat-burning stoves, replacement boilers and furnaces, and hydrogen-fueled equipment.

Renewable Energy Source Expenditures

You may receive an additional energy credit for amounts you spend on solar, wind-powered, or geothermal property for your home. This credit is computed by taking 30% of the first $2,000 and 20% of the next $8,000 of these expenditures. You are eligible for the credit when the original installation of the property is completed. As in the case of energy conservation expenditures, the full $10,000 limit on renewable energy source expenditures may be spread over several tax years. A new $10,000 limit applies for each principal residence you occupy during the period of the credit.

Principal residence. Renewable energy source equipment, such as solar collectors, windmills, or geothermal wells, must be installed for use with your principal residence, which must be located in the United States. However, unlike the credit for energy conservation expenditures, the credit for renewable energy source equipment may be claimed for items installed for use with new, as well as existing, homes. For purposes of the credit it is immaterial when your home was constructed, as long as the renewable energy source property was installed after April 19, 1977.

However, if renewable energy source property is installed during construction or reconstruction of a residence, it is eligible for the credit when you first occupy the residence as your principal residence. Thus, if the property was installed before April 20, 1977, it may qualify for the credit if you first occupied the residence after April 19, 1977. But if you reoccupy a reconstructed dwelling that you had occu-

pied as your principal residence before the reconstruction, the renewable energy source property is eligible for the credit when it is installed. "Reconstruction" is the replacement of most of a dwelling's major structures, such as floors, walls, and ceilings.

For purposes of the credit, a residence is considered your principal residence beginning 30 days before the date you occupy it.

The renewable energy source property, to qualify, must be new, must be expected to last at least 5 years, and must meet certain performance and quality standards to be specified by the Secretary of the Treasury. As of the date of this publication, no performance and quality standards have been issued. However, the property does not need to meet the standards if it is purchased before the standards are published. The cost of renewable energy source equipment includes labor cost properly allocable to the on-site preparation, assembly, or installation of the equipment.

Renewable energy source property includes the following:

Solar energy equipment for heating or cooling a dwelling or for providing hot water for use within the dwelling

Wind energy equipment for generating electricity or other forms of energy for personal residential purposes

Geothermal energy equipment

Additional devices, when specified by the Secretary of the Treasury, that rely on renewable energy sources for heating or cooling a dwelling or for providing hot water for use within the dwelling. As of the date of this publication, no additional devices have been so specified.

A renewable energy source expenditure does not include any expenditure for a swimming pool used as an energy storage medium. Nor does it include an expenditure for an energy storage medium that has a primary function other than the function of energy storage. It also does not include an expenditure for a heating and cooling system to supplement renewable energy source equipment, if the supplementary system uses a form of energy other than solar, wind, or geothermal.

Solar energy property is equipment that uses solar energy to heat or cool a dwelling or to provide hot water for use within the dwelling. Generally, a solar energy system changes sunlight into heat or electricity through the use of equipment such as collectors (to absorb sunlight and create hot air), rockbeds (to store hot air), thermostats (to activate fans that circulate the hot air), and heat exchangers (to utilize hot air to heat water).

Solar energy property includes "passive" solar systems, "active" solar systems, and combinations of both types. An active solar system is based on the use of mechanically forced energy transfer, for example, using fans to circulate solar heat. A passive solar system is based on the use of conductive, convective, or radiant energy transfer, for example, using portions of the structure as solar furnaces to add heat to the structure. However, for purposes of the credit, materials and components that serve a significant structural function, or are structural components, such as extra-thick walls, windows, skylights, greenhouses, and roof overhangs, are not included as solar energy property.

Wind energy property is equipment that uses wind energy to produce energy in any form for personal residential purposes. Generally, wind energy equipment consists of a windmill that generates electricity and mechanical forms of energy. Equipment that uses wind energy for transporation does not qualify.

Geothermal energy property is equipment that uses geothermal energy to heat or cool a dwelling or to provide hot water for use within the dwelling. This is done by distributing or using geothermal deposits. A geothermal deposit is a geothermal reservoir containing natural heat stored in rocks, water, or vapor. For example, hot springs are a geothermal deposit.

How to claim the credit. You claim the credit on line 45 of your Form 1040 for 1978. The amount of credit is computed on Form 5695, *Energy Credits,* which you attach to your return. All eligible expenditures from April 20, 1977, through the end of 1978 are included in computing your credit for 1978. For this purpose, expenditures are generally treated as made when the original installation is completed. You may not amend a 1977 return to claim an energy credit for that year. You may not claim an energy credit on Form 1040A.

If you file your return on a fiscal year basis, you may not take the credit until your first tax year beginning after 1977.

Your residential energy credit must amount to at least $10 in any one year before it may be claimed. This $10 minimum applies *before* you consider the limitation to tax described in the following paragraph. The minimum applies to either joint or separate returns.

The credit may not exceed the amount of tax for which you are otherwise liable. Specifically, it is limited to the tax on line 37, Form 1040, minus the credits on lines 38 through 44, Form 1040.

Carryover of unused credit. You may carry over an unused credit (that you may not use because it exceeds your tax liability) to the next tax year. An unused credit may continue to be carried over to later tax years through 1987. For a fiscal year filer, an unused credit may be carried over through the fiscal year beginning in 1987.

Form **5695**
Department of the Treasury
Internal Revenue Service

Energy Credits
▶ Attach to Form 1040.

1978 ▶

Name(s) as shown on Form 1040

D1530959

Your social security number

Credit Computation

Energy Conservation [...] year 1978 filers, energy conservation property must have been installed after [...] re January 1, 1979. For these expenditures to qualify for the credit, your principal res[...] [...] be been substantially completed before April 20, 1977.

	(a) Description of Item (See Instruction B)	(b) Amount			
1	Insulation				
	Storm (or thermal) windows or doors				
	Caulking or weatherstripping				
	Other (specify) ▶				
2	Total (add amounts on line 1) **2**				
3	Enter 15% of line 2 (but do not enter more than $300) **3**				

Renewable Energy Source Expenditures. For calendar year 1978 filers, renewable energy source property generally must have been installed after April 19, 1977 and before January 1, 1979.

	(a) Description of Item (See Instruction C)	(b) Amount			
4	Solar				
	Geothermal				
	Wind				
5	Total (add amounts on line 4) **5**				
6	Enter 20% of line 5 (but do not enter more than $2,000)	**6**			
7	Enter 10% of line 5 (but do not enter more than $200)	**7**			
8	Total (add lines 3, 6, and 7—if less than $10, enter zero here and on line 10 below)	**8**			
9	Limitation:				
a	Enter tax from Form 1040, line 37 . . . . **9a**				
b	Enter total of lines 38 through 44 from Form 1040 . . . . . **9b**				
c	Subtract line 9b from line 9a (if less than zero, enter zero)	**9c**			
10	Residential energy credit. Enter the smaller of line 8 or line 9c here and on Form 1040, line 45 . .	**10**			

Instructions

A. Who May Claim the Credit.—Calendar year filers must file Form 5695 to claim a credit for energy saving property installed after April 19, 1977 and before January 1, 1979. Even if you installed an item in 1977 (after April 19), you must claim the credit on your 1978 return. Do not file an amended return for 1977.

Taxpayers with fiscal years beginning in 1977 and ending in 1978 may not claim the credit for the 1977–78 tax year. Fiscal year 1978–79 filers may claim the credit by taking into account the period beginning April 20, 1977 and ending on the last day of the tax year.

B. Energy Conservation Property.—Items eligible for the credit are limited to the following:

(1) insulation (fiberglass, cellulose, etc.) for: ceilings, walls, floors, roofs, water heaters, etc.;

(2) exterior storm (or thermal) windows or doors;

(3) caulking or weatherstripping for exterior windows or doors;

(4) a furnace replacement burner which reduces the amount of fuel used;

(5) a device to make flue openings (for a heating system) more efficient;

(6) an electrical or mechanical furnace ignition system which replaces a gas pilot light;

(7) an automatic energy-saving setback thermostat; and

(8) a meter which displays the cost of energy usage.

These items must be installed in or on your principal residence (as defined in Instruction E) after April 19, 1977 and before January 1, 1979 and meet the following tests:

(1) you must be the first person to use the item, and

(2) the item can be expected to remain in use for at least 3 years.

C. Renewable Energy Source Property.— Solar and geothermal energy property may be used to heat or cool your residence (or provide hot water). Solar energy property includes equipment (collectors, rockbeds, and heat exchangers) that transforms sunlight into heat or electricity. Geothermal energy property includes equipment that distributes the natural heat in rocks or water. Wind energy property uses wind to produce energy in any form (generally electricity) for residential purposes.

Renewable energy source property must be installed in connection with your principal residence (as defined in Instruction E) and meet the following tests:

(1) you must be the first person to use the item, and

(2) the item can be expected to remain in use for at least 5 years.

D. Items That Do Not Qualify for the Credit.—Examples are:

(1) carpeting;

(2) drapes;

(3) wood paneling;

(4) exterior siding;

(5) heat pump;

(6) wood or peat fueled residential equipment;

(7) fluorescent replacement lighting system;

(8) hydrogen fueled residential equipment;

(9) equipment using wind energy for transportation;

(10) expenditures for a swimming pool used as an energy storage medium; and

(11) greenhouses.

E. Principal Residence Rules.—The credit is available only for your principal residence (you may either own it or rent it from another person). It must be the main home occupied by you and your family. A summer or vacation home would not qualify. It must be located in the United States. To qualify for the energy conservation credit, the residence must have been substantially completed before April 20, 1977.

Note: Please get Publication 903, Energy Credits for Individuals, for special rules about principal residences.

F. Amount of Credit.—The amount of the credit is based on the cost of the item. The cost of an energy conservation item includes its original installation. The cost of a renewable energy source item includes labor costs for its onsite preparation, assembly, or original installation.

The maximum credit for energy conservation items is $300 for each residence. The maximum credit for renewable energy source items is $2,200 for each residence.

Please get Publication 903 for additional information if you occupied two or more principal residences and made expenditures for energy conservation property or renewable energy source property.

G. Unused Credit Carryover.—If your energy credit for 1978 is more than your tax, you may carry over the unused amount to 1979.

Note: For additional information, get Publication 903, Energy Credits for Individuals.